500

Tips for Quality

Enhancement in

Universities

and Colleges

500 Tips from Kogan Page

500

Tips for Quality Enhancement in Universities and Colleges

SALLY BROWN, PHIL RACE AND BRENDA SMITH

KOGAN PAGE

First published in 1997

Kogan Page Limited
120 Pentonville Road
London N1 9JN
and
22883 Quicksilver Drive
Stirling, VA 20166, USA

British Library Cataloguing in Publication Data

A CIP record for this book is available from the British Library.

ISBN 0 7494 2223 8

Typeset by Jo Brereton, Primary Focus, Haslington, Cheshire
Printed and bound in Great Britain by Clays Ltd, St Ives plc

Contents

Acknowledgements

We are grateful to many colleagues for informal and useful comments on our work towards writing this book. We are particularly indebted to the following for providing deep and helpful feedback on the pilot version:

Hazel Fullerton of the University of Plymouth
Maggy McNorton of the University of Glamorgan
Chris Osborne of Middlesex University
Chris O'Hagan of the University of Derby.

Their valuable suggestions are fully incorporated into the book, and we believe enrich it considerably.

Foreword

Quality in times of change

This book is written to help staff in universities and colleges, at a time when in the UK and many other parts of the world educational institutions are reeling from the effects of unprecedented rates of change, including factors such as:

- growing student numbers without commensurate growth of staffing;
- an increasingly diverse student population;
- the demand to be seen as cost-effective, within frameworks more properly applied to commercial businesses than to educational institutions;
- increasing control by the funding authorities;
- staff who are often demoralised, stressed, and overworked as they try to maintain the quality of what they do, while the circumstances in which they work change.

Our aim in this book is to provide staff with practical and realistic suggestions from which they can select the most appropriate areas through which to address the enhancement of the quality of their own work.

Quality enhancement, or quality assurance?

This book is about quality enhancement, and it is important at the outset to distinguish between this concept and another term which is closely related: quality assurance. At a conference on quality enhancement in 1996 David Melville, former Vice-Chancellor of Middlesex University, proposed that 'the only legitimate product of the quality assurance process is quality enhancement'. With teaching quality assessments (as well as assessments of the quality of research) being used in further and higher education institutions in the UK and in several other parts of the world, there have grown close links in people's minds between quality assurance procedures and funding decisions affecting colleges and universities. While it is essential for institutional survival to fare well in quality assessments, in the long term it is even more important for the quality enhancement product to be realised, and reflected in the quality of the processes of teaching, learning and assessment in colleges and universities.

The keys to effective change include empowering individual members of staff to effect quality enhancement initiatives in their own work, in the context of a collaborative culture. Educational institutions need to be not only places where learning experiences are facilitated for students, but learning organisations in their own right, learning together how best to optimise simultaneously the educational experience for students, and the work experience for staff. This it best achieved when there is an atmosphere of trust, which in turn is more likely to grow when everyone has a shared view of the nature of quality enhancement.

Professor Mantz Yorke has made useful distinctions between quality assurance and quality enhancement, as follows:

Quality Assurance = accountability	*Quality Enhancement = improvement*
Reflects external interests and requirements	Reflects internal interests and values
Depends on inspection	Centres on evaluation
Involves extrinsic motivation	Involves intrinsic motivation
Is subject to external control	Involves empowerment
Focuses on information	Centres on learning

The processes of quality enhancement

Robin Middlehurst, former director of the Higher Education Quality Council in the UK (when it was an agency separate from the funding body) suggested that the following four processes reflect the scope of quality enhancement.

- Explain what you do.

- Do it better (incremental improvement).

- Do it differently (alternative approaches).

- Do it differently and better (transformation).

She emphasised that in the current climate in educational institutions, transformation should be the goal, and that steps towards that goal involve:

- clarifying purposes and responsibilities;

- clarifying tasks, methods and standards;

- paying appropriate attention to the needs of clients and stakeholders;

- undertaking critical self-evaluation;

- exercising imagination, commitment and initiative.

Who should be involved in quality enhancement?

Quality enhancement is not just an issue to be addressed by the senior management of educational institutions. Quality is everyone's business. It is therefore important to engage as wide a cross-section of the staff who work in institutions in proactive analyses of the factors effecting the quality of the work they engage in, and we have written this book to address this need. Our book is intended to be of practical use to individual members of staff, whose work is increasingly impacted upon by quality assurance procedures and quality assessments, to help them effect their own changes to practice, which will contribute to the overall quality enhancement of the work of their institutions.

We wish to emphasise that for any individual member of staff, there are likely to be very many of our suggestions that will already have been not only put into practice, but exceeded upon in their work. There will be other suggestions that are completely outside their spheres of operation, and the implementation of which will depend on other colleagues (academic, administrative, or managerial) in their institutions. However, we believe that everyone working in educational institutions will find in this book some suggestions that will help them to further enhance the overall quality of their work as it relates to teaching, learning and assessment.

Ways of using this book

There are several ways in which to use this book, including:

- as an aid to undertaking a personal quality audit of the various dimensions of your work, taking pleasure in all those aspects where you have already exceeded our suggestions, and looking for areas you may address next;

- to provide agenda for discussion by course teams, looking towards enhancing the overall quality of the teaching, learning and assessment in particular courses and disciplines;

- as a resource for your school or department, to help prepare for success in quality assessments, and to ensure that the quality enhancement product of such assessments is addressed constructively;

- as a framework against which to formulate departmental or institutional quality assurance mechanisms.

Chapter 1   Valuing Students

There is no single starting place for a book on quality enhancement for educational contexts, but the greatest potential benefits undoubtedly belong to our students. With growing student numbers in many courses, and with greater diversity among the student population, and with increased and more demanding expectations from students, it is imperative that the quality of their experience of higher education is addressed. This does not solely involve their experience in teaching–learning contexts, but the cumulative experience from induction to graduation. Furthermore, many of the aspects of quality enhancement we have addressed in this chapter are quite visible, and therefore are sources of evidence that are likely to be seen by all of the stakeholders in our educational institutions, and by quality assessors/reviewers.

We start with some suggestions about student induction. For our students, this is their first impression of the quality of the way we go about our work. We have limited ourselves to what we think are some key starting points towards enhancing the quality of student induction processes.

Next, we turn to one of the most visible forms of evidence of the quality of student induction: student handbooks. With larger numbers of students and fewer members of staff, students do not have as much opportunity as once was the case to talk to staff and ask questions about their courses. Much of the help we wish to give students now has to be encapsulated in formats such as student handbooks. We hope that our suggestions will help you to ensure that student handbooks are useful companions to students during their courses, rather than something they skim through once then file, never to be seen again.

We next turn our attention to mature students. In many institutions, the proportion of mature students continues to grow. Indeed, there is much to be said for treating all of our students as mature people, but it is particularly important not to treat our mature students inappropriately. We then move on to some suggestions about specific provision for part-time students, who make up a large part of the growth in mature students. The time that such students spend in our institutions is much more limited, and it is therefore important to ensure that the quality of their experience during this time is enhanced in every way we can.

Our next set of suggestions addresses some of the needs of students from overseas. The proportion of such students varies considerably from one institution to another, and across different disciplines. We need to cater appropriately for them throughout our teaching, learning and assessment work, but in this section we offer some suggestions about meeting the special needs that are often crucially important to them, especially at the outset of their studies in our institutions.

We then turn our attention to the other end of the timescale, and offer some suggestions about graduation processes. It is important that our students' educational experience does not just fizzle out, but comes to a memorable and worthy conclusion. In addition, graduation events are a very public indicator of the quality of our institutions, and enhancing this quality is something that is noticed by all of the stakeholders in higher education.

We end this chapter by looking beyond graduation. Gone are the days when a degree was a passport to a lifetime's career, and more and more graduates are coming back into our institutions, either straightaway to do a further programme of advanced study or research, or later in their lives for professional updating and further qualifications. Where these students choose to continue their education depends not least on the quality of the ways in which we treat them when they return, and our suggestions are designed to help you make your institution a preferred choice for them.

1

Enhancing quality through student induction

It is tough learning how to be an effective student. For many, it is their first time away from home and for most it involves developing a whole new way of studying, often with more independence and autonomy than any are used to. It can be a wonderfully exciting time, but also a frightening and worrying one. We need to do everything we can to help our students settle in, not only because we want to offer a humane and professional environment but also because low retention rates are a sign of a poor institution as well as a terrible waste of time, money, effort and student morale. These tips aim to offer some pointers on how we can welcome newcomers and help them feel a part of the academic community.

1 **Help students to get to know each other.** Use some of the innumerable icebreaking activities available to break down barriers and help the students to become acquainted. If possible, get them to know and use each other's names at every opportunity.

2 **Help them to find their way around.** We tend to forget how large and daunting the institutions we work in can seem to newcomers, especially if they are returning to study after a long gap or if they have come from a relatively small institution. Help them with maps, with orientation sessions, with interactive CDs or videos if available.

3 **Avoid information overload, and get students learning-by-doing.** Try not to shower students with too many pieces of paper too soon. Avoid giving them important information in forms that are easy to lose, like handouts that look like all the other handouts. Stage the giving out of key data and provide it in a collated form if possible. Structure induction processes so that students are involved in activities as soon as possible, preferably in groups of two or three, so no one is left alone.

4   **Address students' expectations.** Some of them may prefer to be spoon-fed, and need to be reminded that they may now be reading for a degree, where more of the responsibility for developing their self-awareness, sense of motivation, and taking on challenges lies with them.

5   **Find them buddies.** Many institutions find ways of pairing or grouping new students with those who have been around a while. Having a fellow student to turn to can be a real bonus for those students who do not wish to feel stupid by asking damn fool questions or who find themselves unconfident in the face of high-powered academics.

6   **Give them a good guidebook.** These are often best written by other students, who usually have a good idea of what students need to know. The tone of the guidebook should be light without being patronising, informative but not dull. To achieve this is no mean feat!

7   **Help them learn to study.** For many, the terminology of academic life can be a closed book. Unless you tell them what you expect them to do in a seminar or in directed study, they may be confused. They may also need plenty of advice about what to do in lectures, how they should tackle assignments, how to prepare for and cope with exams, what to buy on a reading list and how to work effectively in groups.

8   **Make induction fun.** Be always alert for ways to motivate students to get to know about their new learning environment. Treasure hunts can be a great way of finding your way around a campus, for example, and making these activities group ones can help students to get to know each other better.

9   **Make use of existing students.** Second- and third-year students know the place and the systems – maybe better than you do from students' perspectives. Get them to help you not only carry out induction activities, but also to design them.

10 **Think about equal opportunities**. Freshers' pub crawls or cheese and wine sessions might seem to be really good ways of getting to know each other, but can make students from cultures where alcohol is frowned on rather uncomfortable. Similarly, some students will be made really uncomfortable by the levels of body contact required in some of the physical ice-breaker games. After-hours sessions can be equally problematic for students with caring commitments.

11 **Support their information needs.** Induct students in how to use the library, how to use the open-access IT centres, where to go for counselling and accommodation advice, who will help them when they have money problems and what to do if they think they are on the wrong course.

12 **Evaluate your induction.** Keep monitoring how your students have experienced induction and really listen to what they tell you. It will help you to devise programmes that are student-centred, appropriate and valuable.

13 **Keep induction going.** Don't try to do it all in the first week. Different topics need induction at different stages, especially things that are important regarding the transition from one year of a programme of study to the next.

2

Student handbooks

Student handbooks are often the first substantial printed materials that students receive on a course or module. They set the tone for the quality of the whole course, and are also indicators to quality assessors/reviewers and other outside agencies. The provision of useful and informative student handbooks is now considered by many to be essential to good practice, and increasingly handbooks are being taken to be a quality indicator both for particular courses, and for institutions as a whole. The following suggestions may help you to ensure that your student handbooks are good ambassadors both for your courses and your institution.

1   **Work out what sort of handbook provision you intend to make.** Some institutions have a policy of providing student handbooks for entire courses, while others provide handbooks for particular modules. Where students will be provided with a range of different handbooks, it is as important not to duplicate all sorts of general information as it is to make sure that such general information (such as assessment regulations and procedures) is provided to every student once. Where an institution-wide handbook is issued during induction, this can serve as a basis upon which individual course or module handbooks can build, avoiding wasteful replication of general information.

2   **Decide on the purposes to be served by student handbooks.** These may include informing, amusing and encouraging. Decide whether it is something to be written into by students, or to be added to during the course. Careful thinking about the roles you wish the handbooks to fulfil can help to ensure that they will be well used. It is also important to decide whether the handbooks are going to be designed to relate to individual modules, whole courses, or an entire programme of study. Loose-leaf formats have the advantage that separate module handbooks can be produced and incorporated into a specific collection of handbook elements by students studying different combinations of modules.

3   **Keep handbooks relatively simple.** Students tend to be bombarded with information at the start of a programme. If the handbook contains too much information, or is poorly organised, the contents will not be used.

4   **Involve students in handbook design.** They (and only they) really know which information proves useful. Think about running a competition for students for the best design specification of a handbook, and the most appropriate listing of what it should (and should not) contain. Consider involving students who may already be running student magazines. Try to make the handbook indispensable, for example by giving it an extra purpose, such as being a diary as well, and maybe containing useful study-skills guidance suggestions. Try to include some fun in student handbooks, such as cartoons, quotes, illustrations, quizzes or competitions.

5   **Double-check the information.** It is only too easy for once-correct information to become outdated, yet continue to be reproduced in student handbooks. Even incorrect telephone numbers can be frustrating. Have someone responsible for each entry in the course handbook, and send them a copy of their bit of the last one, to edit and amend, when asking for the next edition. Give realistic deadlines to maximise the chance that editing will be done well.

6   **Keep handbooks up to date on an annual basis.** All sorts of things may change, including assessment regulations, opening times of libraries, refectories and buildings, grant conditions, and computing services provision and regulations.

7   **Be clear about production costs.** Going in for a professionally produced handbook can be an attractive option, but a sensible cost-benefit analysis should be undertaken. A home-produced handbook can be easier to update, even mid-programme, while a professional-looking one brings advantages of credibility and enhancement to the ethos of a course.

8   **Work out distribution mechanisms.** Some institutions organise the distribution of student handbooks centrally. It is important to ensure that on split-site campuses the supply of student handbooks is right, and that they get to the students! Consider a 'give and take' process, such as issuing the handbooks on receipt of an essential enrolment form.

9   **Consider using more than one format.** Suitable software is available for making it easy to produce a networked electronic form of a course handbook, or for it to be issued to students on computer disks of their own. However, it may be necessary to run printed and electronic versions in parallel for some time to ensure that *all* students have appropriate access to the information involved.

10   **Think of the quality that students now expect.** Students are now exposed to high-quality desktop published material with graphics, and institutions often have standards of production for anything that could be an ambassador of the quality of the institution. Some components of any student handbook may be shared across an institution, and economies of scale of production of these can be achieved.

11   **Evaluate the success of student handbooks.** It is important to gather feedback about how student handbooks are used, and what students would like added – or removed – from them. Include a feedback form in handbooks, to be sent to a named person who will be responsible for collecting and analysing the information provided in student feedback. A prize draw from completed feedback forms can be a low-cost way of encouraging student participation.

3

Making mature students feel welcome

We've all seen mature students who revel in returning to student life, and revert happily to their youth – or to the student life they missed out on previously. However, many mature students feel quite intimidated and uneasy at the prospect of returning to college and perhaps being the senior citizens in a student group. The following suggestions are made on their behalf.

1   **Remember that mature students may know a lot!** Their work experience may have equipped them with knowledge of how some of the topics they are studying relate to the real world, and it's worth giving them the chance to share this experience. This can do a lot to increase their confidence in the group.

2   **Mature students tend to be over-anxious.** They often take their studying a lot more seriously than some of their younger counterparts – one reason being that they are often footing the bill themselves, or are being invested in by their employers. They also tend to return to education with the more serious attitudes that may have been prevalent when they were last in an education system. Helping them overcome such anxiety can be a major step to developing their confidence in their ability to succeed, which in turn is probably one of the most significant factors predetermining their success.

3   **Remember that mature students don't know everything – or may be 'rusty'!** This is the other side of the point made in the previous tip. Just because mature students look older doesn't automatically mean that they have been taught some of the things that their younger counterparts have learned. There will be gaps, and it is important to ensure that mature students find out about these gaps with minimum embarrassment. Similarly, mature students may be out of practice in some academic skills

such as essay writing or note taking. It can be useful to offer 'refresher' tips to groups of mature students before anyone reveals any such shortcomings.

4   **Take care about assumptions.** Some mature students will have covered ground you might never have expected them to have done, and others won't have experienced things you would have expected them to have covered. It's well worth spending a little time finding out a bit more about mature students' views of their own strengths and weaknesses.

5   **Consider designing a self-profiling questionnaire for all of your students.** This can give you an accurate picture of where the skills and competences of your mature students and their younger classmates overlap or diverge.

6   **Check out the expectations of your mature students.** Ask them why they have chosen to study your subject, and how they believe it will fit into their future careers. They will often have more definite answers to these questions than younger students who are simply taking your subject because it is part of their whole course.

7   **Treat mature students appropriately.** They do not like being treated like children – but of course neither do younger students – or children themselves! It is worth reminding yourself that most mature students who are just learners in your classroom are likely to be experienced professionals like yourself in other places. Be sensitive about the different focus that mature students need regarding their first week or two on a course; unlike some 18-year-olds, their priority is not likely to be to devote that phase of their course to enjoying alcohol!

8   **Help mature students to save face.** Mature people often don't like to be seen to get things wrong, especially when seen by younger people. Watch out for occasions when feedback from assessments may raise this issue.

9   **Give mature students the chance to interact well with the rest of the group.** When choosing groups for tasks or projects, it is often worth trying to get a good mix regarding age and background, to allow exchange of knowledge and experience in as many directions as possible.

10 **Be realistic about other demands on mature students' time and energy.** They normally have abundant motivation and drive, but sometimes other pressures in their lives can affect the possibility of them meeting deadlines or targets.

11   **Be a mature student yourself!** It is always useful to put yourself in a position similar to that of your students. Even if the course or topic you're studying is a minor part of your life, being a learner again will alert you to ways of refreshing your own teaching practice.

12   **Suggest the formation of a Mature Students' Group.** This can provide not only moral support and social activities, but may be able to give practical help to mature students through the organisation of grants, rebates, and focused help on the problems most likely to be encountered by such students.

4

Providing for part-time students

Universities and colleges have experienced a major shift towards the provision of part-time courses for students, and this trend is certain to continue, with greater numbers of people requiring professional updating programmes and mid-career retraining. The following suggestions should help to ensure that the quality of provision for part-timers is enhanced.

1   **Remember that part-time students aren't full-time students!** In particular, they have not got the time to spend on unproductive activities such as waiting around, queuing, sorting out administrative details, and other things that can be done easily by full-time students in between classes and lectures. As part-time students have less chance to solve problems with course documentation by talking to each other, ensure that all written guides and instructions that they use are particularly clear and un-ambiguous.

2   **Part-time students usually have cars!** Make provision for part-timers to have the chance to apply for restricted parking permits, such as 'Wednesday Only'. Lack of equal treatment regarding car parking often makes part-time students feel like second-class citizens even before they get to their classes.

3   **Think carefully about the starting-time for part-time sessions.** For example, when classes for part-timers start at 10.00, it may be impossible for them to find anywhere to park their cars, as everywhere will already be full. Coming in at 08.20 to park means wasting a lot of their precious time, or if they call in at their workplace before coming to college they may well be delayed or prevented from coming altogether by pressing demands. Consider timing the start of part-time sessions early, and even *before* normal full-time classes commence.

4   **Have special library arrangements to suit part-timers.** This can include arranging priority status for short-loans on selected key texts for part-time students, and library hours that allow them to come in after work or at weekends.

5   **Make face-to-face time as relevant as possible for part-time students.** In particular, make sure that they are not sitting passively listening to things they already know. Check out at the beginning of each topic to find out what the existing knowledge base is in the group, and prioritise your agenda accordingly. Use face-to-face time for things where part-timers really need a shared experience. Part-time students have less opportunity to talk to each other than full-timers, and we need to make sure that they get as much feedback from each other as we can arrange, during the times the group is together.

6   **Choose the topics well for class sessions.** Use valuable contact time to address subjects where part-timers are likely to need your expertise. This means choosing to spotlight important parts of the syllabus, and dealing with these in depth, rather than trying to run through the whole syllabus during limited contact time.

7   **Make it easy for part-timers to work on their own through appropriate parts of the syllabus.** Turn notes, handouts, and other learning resources into effective self-study materials, so that part-timers can make their own way through topics that don't normally cause problems.

8   **Making video recordings of key lectures, seminars or tutorials can be a real benefit to part-time students.** When they miss a session unavoidably, they can catch up very significantly if it is possible for them to see exactly what they missed. It is therefore worth considering making sure that there is an alternative way for part-timers to capture particularly important course sessions.

9   **Don't assume that part-time students have out-of-hours access to facilities.** All of their in-college time is likely to be timetabled in classes. If they will require information technology facilities for work to be handed in for assessment, they may need a longer lead-in time to allow them to arrange access to such facilities.

10   **Lack of refreshments provision can be a real problem.** Many part-timers arrive on campus after a busy time at their workplace, and without having had the chance to get anything to eat or drink. When campus facilities offer only limited provision, part-timers can end up hungry and de-hydrated – not the best state to learn effectively. Moreover, good catering provision helps part-timers to congregate together and talk before or after sessions, and the learning payoff of such interaction is highly significant.

11   **Part-time students may need the same sorts of help as full-time students.**
Support services such as counselling and personal tutoring can be just as
crucial for part-time as for full-time students. Problems can remain
unsolved if the support provision does not extend to times when part-
timers can make use of it.

12   **Take particular care regarding referred reading and set coursework.** Part-
timers may not have the time to read widely, and it helps them a lot if you
make references quite specific, indicating to them exactly what you intend
them to derive from their work with each source. Because of the other
demands on their time, it is important that part-time students are given
plenty of notice of deadlines for assessed coursework, and allowed
additional leeway if they are finding it hard to meet particular deadlines.

13   **Use alternative means of communication for part-timers.** For example,
use internal mail for question-and-answer communication between
yourself and part-time students, and (for those students with access to
appropriate facilities) make the most of e-mail and computer conferencing
possibilities. Consider having a telephone helpline, say daily from 18.30-
19.30, when someone is available in the office to pick up problems and
reassure students.

14   **Keep part-time students informed.** Find systems for letting them know
about changes to timetables, or other changes which are often last-minute
ones. They hate travelling in only to find that their lecture that day has
been rearranged or cancelled!

5

Providing for overseas students

We should state firmly at the outset of these suggestions that we are not just thinking about overseas students. This term is often used in the UK (for example) when also meaning students from different race or ethnic backgrounds who may not be from another country, or who may be learning in English as a second or other language (ESOL students is a more acceptable acronym). Different universities work with different proportions of such students. The following suggestions could provide a starting agenda for your own discussions on how best to enhance the quality of the experience of such students.

1   **Arrange specialist induction provision for overseas students.** Pre-sessional classes addressing aspects of cultural acclimatisation, and study skills, can be of enormous benefit in helping such students start off their academic studies without being disadvantaged.

2   **Produce clear information for overseas students.** Ideally we should be producing clear information for all students, for example through course handbooks, but it is particularly important that overseas students should receive good documentation about their courses, as well as about the institution and its environs. Overseas students are more likely to need to revisit such information again and again until they have tuned in to their new situation, and they can often do this more successfully when the information is in print rather than in easy-to-forget face-to-face formats.

3   **Help students from other countries or cultures to understand what is expected of them in assessment.** Assessment cultures vary widely round the world, and what is regarded as normal practice in some places is seen as cheating or plagiarism in others. It is important that all students are aware of the ways they are expected to behave in preparing for and undertaking any kind of assessment. It can be particularly important to help students adjust to those parts of their courses involving independent study, and about how to prepare for the assessment associated with such studies.

4   **Search for ways of lessening the isolation of overseas students.**
    Encourage them out of the institution, so they can absorb more of the
    local culture, and make new contacts and friends.

5   **Be sensitive on issues of religion.** Some religions require followers to
    pray at specific times and in particular settings. This can be a problem for
    students required to fit in with tight timetabling, and sensitive flexibility
    needs to be shown regarding their needs and rights.

6   **Help students with special food requirements.** Coping with a new culture
    is enough of a hurdle for students from different backgrounds and cultures,
    without imposing the additional burden of having to cope with 'majority'
    food habits. Gather feedback on acceptable alternatives that could be built
    into menus and catering provision. Advise those arranging catering at
    induction events to be especially sensitive about labelling food, so that
    international students don't become anxious about what they can and
    cannot eat.

7   **Consider getting previous students from each country to write an
    introductory guide to the idiosyncrasies of the British!** It can be useful
    for new students from overseas – and for staff and students not from
    abroad – to get the chance to see ourselves through the eyes of people
    from other countries.

8   **Be sensitive about alcohol.** This does not just mean expecting groups of
    students, whatever their background, to go on field trips or visits which
    include a stop on the way back at a suitable pub! Class discussions of
    alcohol marketing strategies or pub social behaviours will be offensive or
    alien to students whose culture forbids alcohol.

9   **Consider the special facilities needed by students from other countries.**
    For example, toilet and washing facilities need to accommodate the
    different practices that are involved in some cultures or religions. When
    such students attempt to make use of 'normal' facilities, their actions are
    in danger of being misunderstood.

10 **Consider the accommodation needs of students from other cultures.**
    For example, students from some countries, when booking their place at
    university in the UK, may not know what is meant by 'hall of residence',
    'single-study-bedroom' or 'shared student apartment'. Accommodation
    literature needs to be written or supplemented so that all students know
    what each category of accommodation entails.

11   **Offer language support at appropriate levels.** Students studying in English as a second or other language will need different kinds of language support as they continue their studies. At first, they may need help in getting started in English, but later the help they need may be more connected to how they should use written language in assessed work, and spoken English in interviews with tutors or in oral examinations.

12   **Help them to communicate with home, especially in emergencies.** International telephone or fax charges are high, and students may not have access to locations where they can use such communications in relative privacy. The costs, both financial and academic, of students having to make emergency visits home are more serious, and ways need to be found of helping students sort out some of the problems that could lead them into such costs.

13   **Help them to understand what is expected of them in seminars.** Many overseas students come from cultures with particularly formal methods of education, and find it hard to cope with the more interactive modes of teaching. Students from some cultures can find it a shock to encounter the full and frank debates between students and tutors which are regarded as healthy indicators of a seminar. This may explain their own reluctance to become involved, and they will need patient encouragement to adopt the roles that they are expected to play in their new setting.

6

Graduation

Never underestimate the value of graduation. Students, their friends and relatives all look forward to the event. New outfits, extra camera film and restaurant bookings are all parts of these important days – as well as the hope for fine weather. Here are some suggestions for enhancing the quality of graduation ceremonies.

1   **Set the date well in advance.** It is never too early to get such dates into diaries. Remember some parents may have to book annual leave a year in advance. Ensure dates do not clash with major external events such as sporting fixtures, which could lead to divided loyalties, and congested routes if such events are local.

2   **Book appropriate 'other' rooms.** Space to change into academic dress, places to shelter from inclement weather, suitable locations for photographs to be taken are all required. Where will all the university souvenirs be sold? Where will graduands meet their friends? Think also about eating arrangements – a welcome hot or cold drink on arrival is much welcomed.

3   **Organise crèche facilities so that little ones do not disturb the ceremony!** Graduation tends for many students to be a family event, and crèche facilities are often available in the institution for regular students and staff. It is worth going that bit extra to arrange some extra provision on graduation days.

4   **Allow places and times for graduands to mingle.** They will be keen to renew acquaintances with their former fellow students, and also to say 'goodbye' for maybe the last time to some of their friends.

5   **Organise university gifts and souvenirs.** People want all sorts of things: something for the scrapbook or a university mug can become treasured possessions. Display goods where they are visible without impeding circulation, making sure price tags are clearly visible. Check that credit cards and cheques can be processed readily, and have a plentiful supply of small change in the till.

6   **Liaise with the local press and local TV and radio.** For example, time the production of an educational supplement to coincide with the ceremonies. The marketing or promotional people come into their own here. Worthy of a mention in such supplements are memorable events, special awards, links with overseas projects, as well as lists of graduands and diplomates. Such supplements often get put into the 'This is Your Life' album! Highlights from the speeches made by important visitors can be of interest to local TV and radio audiences, and arranging interviews for the celebrities can be good publicity, as well as making the celebrities feel even more celebrated!

7   **Celebrate with supporting events.** These can take forms such as street theatre, a string quartet, jazz band, and not least the famous (or infamous) Graduation Ball. A festive atmosphere, well planned, with possibilities of inclement weather duly considered, can help the alumni figures.

8   **Capture interest before the ceremony begins.** Guests often have to be in their seats well before the ceremony starts. Entertain them or inform them with a slide-show or multimedia display. High-quality visuals and music can add to the ambience. Avoid, however, having graduation events which are too long. Break them into sections, with different honorary awards at different times. Spreading these out between ceremonies can add to the interest for parents and graduates, such as when an honoured guest makes a memorable speech.

9   **Record the event for posterity.** Now with the latest technology 'The Video!' can be available for all immediately after the ceremony. People find these good to look back on, not least to discuss the fashions of the day, and are especially welcomed by those relatives who may be unable to attend for whatever reasons.

10   **Think about exporting the pomp and ceremony.** When there are very significant numbers of students from particular overseas countries, such as with large-scale franchise arrangements, it can be more cost-effective to take the fancy dress (and the mace!) to them, rather than bringing all of the students to the home institution. Such exported events can usefully be coupled with student recruitment drives at the locations involved – the visible signs of the ceremony celebrating academic success are good for creating more demand.

11 **Publicise alumni – 'it's good to keep in touch'.** Alumni organisations can keep people informed, keep them in contact, and ask them for donations. It is essential that databases are set up and maintained on a regular basis. Use alumni to capture their feedback on their experience, and the implications of that experience for higher education to take on board for the benefit of future graduates.

12 **Promote opportunities for lifelong learning.** At a graduation ceremony there is a captive audience. Students just qualified may not feel like registering for that Masters or PhD yet, but after a few months or years away from that rich learning environment, they may feel the need to return. Some parents or friends may be hooked on the day. Liaise with alumni about future course development.

13 **Reflect.** There may be exhaustion, expense and even tension on the day, but is the end result happy graduands? Obtain feedback from staff involved. Could there be better liaison next year? Were any certificates lost? Was the catering good? Did everyone get a gown? Listen to conversations during the day, and feed back the main points noted to a central source. Don't forget to ask the graduates themselves too.

7

Getting people to come back

Long gone are the days when a degree or a diploma set people up for a lifetime's career in their chosen discipline. Today's world requires people who can keep up with rapidly changing situations, and who can move from one field to another at short notice. The people who fare best are those who remain active learners. The following suggestions may help to avoid putting people off being lifelong learners!

1   **Make time to address study skills.** In many ways, learning to learn effectively is one of the most important outcomes of successful educational experiences. It is unwise to assume that everyone automatically knows how to learn effectively.

2   **Don't marginalise learning skills development.** This is not something to leave to some so-called experts running study-skills programmes. The best people to engender effective studying techniques are the subject teachers themselves, who can relate learning strategies to the particular nature of each discipline and topic.

3   **Do everything possible to make learning an enjoyable and satisfying experience for students.** People are much more likely to return for more if they enjoy their first helpings.

4   **Consider options which may cause students to keep contact after their courses finish.** Life-membership (or fixed long-term membership) of students' unions is often available to students, but it is worth considering arrangements for long-term membership of libraries, learning resources centres, computer network groups, and so on. When students are in regular contact with the college after they finish their courses, there is much more chance they will return to further study.

5   **Make alumni associations work.** Too often such arrangements are marginal and ad hoc. Combining at least some of the alumni events with things that involve existing students can help to promote the idea that alumni can continue to take part in major college events. Also, the interactions between past and present students can be very worthwhile. Collect from alumni their thoughts about what turned out to be useful to them in their jobs, and what else would have helped them.

6   **Help to make college environments a pleasant place for students to come to.** The cost of providing comfortable working, eating and relaxing spaces may cause problems in times of limited budgets and overcrowded facilities, but there is a payoff in terms of students returning for further study rather than going elsewhere when they need to develop their careers further.

7   **Develop open learning materials to use with college-based students.** This not only helps to add variety for full-time students, but also helps pave the way towards being able to offer particular modules on a distance-learning basis, or gives part-time students a means of making better use of their limited face-to-face time on campus.

8   **Keep contacts with past students.** This is not something every lecturer can do alongside all the other pressures on them, but every little helps. More globally, keep abreast of what your college may be doing along the lines of alumni associations and newsletters to past students, and contribute when possible to events or publications.

9   **Keep an eye on market needs.** Ask returning students for ideas about further short courses which they would like, and look for trends. Ask employers about the sorts of training they use most regularly. Investigate whether you can collaborate with employers in providing elements of training on-site for them.

10 **Give credit where credit's due.** It is important that everything 'counts' in some way. Credit accumulation and transfer schemes (CATS) are widely developed in most education and training sectors, and the fact that they are working towards some credit points can help ensure that returning students don't drop out when the going gets tougher.

11 **Give due recognition to the value of coming back into higher education after some time out.** Students coming into the system with some life and work experience are often more highly motivated, and have useful experience to draw on and to bring to bear on their education.

Chapter 2   Valuing Staff

The greatest resource to any educational institution is its staff. Staff in many institutions feel overstretched, stressed and devalued by many of the changes that have affected them in recent years. The factors driving change continue, and our next chapter looks at ways of enhancing the quality of our provision by paying attention to the needs and aspirations of teaching staff. In particular, it is important not to pretend that the symptoms of stress produced by rapid change do not exist, but to accept them and look for ways of addressing both the symptoms and some of the causes.

We start with the same processes that we looked at when thinking about students coming into our institutions: induction. As with students, first impressions count a great deal, and the experience which new staff gain during their first few weeks is crucial in establishing a culture of quality enhancement. Academic staff are, however, more demanding in that they need to feel that good use is being made of their time during induction processes or events, as they are usually particularly hard-pressed preparing for imminent teaching duties.

We move next to staff training, which is often associated with probationary conditions in staff appointments, but which needs to be ongoing for all teaching staff. The quality of the provision of staff training should be such that staff gain ideas from the training processes, as well as the content, that enable them to enhance the quality of their own teaching work with students. Staff training provision is also a visible source of evidence, of interest to quality assessors/ reviewers and other parties making decisions about the relative quality of different institutions, not least for funding purposes.

Appraisal systems vary enormously from one institution to another. Appraisal should be a process the outcomes of which feed directly into quality enhancement. However, appraisal should also, when working effectively, be a process involving recognition of the things that academic staff do well, and a celebration of their achievements rather than a diagnosis of their needs for improvement. We offer some straightforward suggestions to help appraisal achieve positive outcomes both for staff and for the institution.

We have already indicated that staff in educational institutions are often stressed and overworked, and seemingly more so with every new change in a rapidly changing system. The remaining suggestions in this chapter aim to help colleagues recognise the sorts of stress that may be affecting their work, as well as to accommodate and tackle the causes of such stress. Our tips about managing stress link into our next set of suggestions, about maintaining morale in institutions. While it may not be possible to offer financial incentives, we explore several other ways of enhancing the vital feeling of collegiality which can help to raise morale. Our final set of suggestions is about 'Coping with turbulent times'. These tips are addressed particularly to individuals who are finding the nature of their work changing faster than feels comfortable.

8

Enhancing quality through staff induction

The way in which institutions of higher education introduce new staff to the organisation, its mission, its practices and its policies, will have important effects on the ultimate quality of the services you provide, as well as affecting how staff feel about the place where they work. These tips aim to offer advice on how you can induct staff effectively, so they become engaged and committed as early as possible.

1   **Induct early.** It isn't always possible to give everyone a proper induction as soon as they start with you, but try to ensure that you have a staged programme, so that you cover the basics pretty rapidly, with follow-up as soon as possible thereafter. Not everyone arrives in September, so a rolling induction programme is desirable.

2   **Welcome newcomers professionally.** Can you be sure that new employees know where to go on the first day, who to report to, where to go for a cup of tea or a meal, where the toilets are, whether they can smoke, who to ask for help, how and when they will be paid? Do they have the equipment (desk, phone, computer, tools or whatever) they need to enable them to start working?

3   **Induct everyone.** Check that your institutional induction programme covers all categories of staff, so that everyone learns about the organisation and where they fit into it. Too often, part-timers, people on short-term contracts, researchers, manual workers and others are missed out of the induction process.

4 **Help them learn the geography.** Give them maps and, if time permits, show them round the campus(es) on foot or in a bus. If you have widely distributed buildings, show them pictures or let them loose on a virtual campus, navigating with a mouse rather than on foot.

5 **Introduce them to people.** Involve members of senior management if they are willing, since inductees often really value the chance to meet the important people in an organisation. Make use of contributions from representatives from central departments like the library and IT services as well as union reps and people like Equal Opportunities officers and representatives from personnel. Organise tours of key service departments, for example reprographics, media services, and student residential facilities.

6 **Use visuals.** If people can't be present in person, can you show (recent, friendly-looking) pictures of key figures either on slides, photos or digitally? Can you use an institutional publicity video to let them see the people and places that you can't cover within the programme?

7 **Make induction fun.** It's really easy to bore inductees to death by making them listen to talking heads all day. Find ways to give them information that don't always involve them being told things. Build in quizzes perhaps, where they have to find out information from a range of paper materials on display or get them into teams to introduce themselves to each other.

8 **Keep them busy.** Give inductees things to do. Try to vary the pace, build in a range of activities, change the venue for part of the session. Give them the chance to prepare questions to ask the speakers during different elements of induction.

9 **Don't forget departmental induction.** Consider providing section leaders, heads of department and others with checklists so that new starters find out what they need to know locally, such as how to organise photocopying, who to go to for signatures and so on, and suggestions about how to start and maintain their own filing systems. It may be useful to have named induction coordinators at local level, who can provide a useful support network to each other.

10 **Point new staff towards ongoing staff development provision.** When the institution runs something along the lines of a Postgraduate Certificate in Educational Development, staff induction can be usefully coupled with an introduction to the nature and scope of such provision, as well as giving new staff the chance to meet the educational developers of the institution.

11 **Help new staff to understand the jargon.** It can be useful to give them a glossary of educational terms and acronyms, and abbreviations used in course documentation. It is worth maintaining such a glossary on the computer network so that it can be maintained continuously and updated.

12 **Feed them!** New staff can be made to feel welcomed and valued in a measure linked to the quality of the catering at staff induction events.

13 **Evaluate your induction.** Ask inductees at the end of the process how they found the programme and use the feedback to continuously improve the way in which you carry out induction.

9

Enhancing the quality of training

Most institutions have a Staff Development or Educational Development Unit of one kind or another, which usually operates with a small number of staff. As all areas in large institutions increasingly become accountable for their own actions, it is important that the training provided for staff at all levels is of high quality, and is tuned well in to the mission and ethos of the institution. The following suggestions may help to promote training of an appropriate level.

1   **Ensure that staff know of the central provision for training.** It is worth thinking carefully about how to publicise training programmes and events, so that the relevant material reaches all staff. The time taken to pre-label the material with individual names can help to prevent such wasteful occurrences as large quantities of material lying around unread in staff rooms.

2   **Training needs to be targeted appropriately.** The training provision which is offered needs to match carefully local and central needs of the institution. Training needs are best analysed by visiting each department and talking to key personnel. Many training needs come to light through the operations of an effective institutional staff appraisal system.

3   **The needs of all categories of staff should be recognised.** Traditionally, the emphasis has been placed on the needs of academic members of staff. However, technical, secretarial, administrative and maintenance staff are all players in an organisation, and the morale and ethos of the institution is enhanced by treating all staff as worthy of investment through training. It is important to ensure that they are all introduced equally at training events, and given the opportunity to get to know people from other departments. Training should be a process which helps to break up departmental or functional cliques.

4   **Training provision should be as flexible as possible.** Staff are busier than ever, and find it increasingly difficult to attend lengthy training events. It is worth thinking of including in training and support provision such features as drop-in events, surgeries, help-desks and online support.

5   **Consider the advantages of awaydays.** Taking staff away from the institution for important training events not only removes them from the everyday distractions which can interrupt a home-based training event, but makes staff feel more valued, and gives a sense of added value to the topic of the training event.

6   **All training programmes need to be evaluated.** It is unwise to rely on any single method of evaluation. Even though written answers to questionnaires are the basis of the most common method of gathering feedback, this feedback may only be instant reactions rather than reflective views. Follow-up focus groups can elicit very useful additional inform-ation, but are time-consuming to carry out, and need to be targeted appropriately.

7   **Staff training programmes should be accredited where possible.** Where a cluster of training programmes are provided for a specific group of staff, it is worth considering putting them together as a package and accrediting them. The qualification resulting from the training could, for example, constitute a University Certificate, or a National Vocational Qualification (NVQ).

8   **Balance the use of internal and external training providers.** It is quite common for it to be possible to get a bigger audience for a distinguished trainer from outside the institution, as for an equally distinguished home-based trainer. Sometimes messages received from outside the institution are taken more seriously than from someone who works there all the time.

9   **Quality guidelines should be provided for visiting trainers or presenters.** These could accompany such correspondence as maps, parking details, and so on, but go on to suggest ground rules for expressing intended learning outcomes, facilitating participative workshops, and using and building on the specific experiences and expertise of the staff being trained.

10   **The quality of training materials is an indicator of the quality of training.** Scrappy or poorly-presented materials that have obviously been used for the last ten years do not give confidence to workshop participants or to anyone else investigating the quality of training in the institution. When external training providers supply copies of materials for reproduction before a training event, it should be policy to return them, or find a better alternative if they are not of an appropriate standard.

11   **Training rooms should be appropriately equipped.** Common signs of poor training provision include overhead projectors which can no longer be focused, flip charts with no blank paper, and video players with missing remote control devices. Even when everything is checked to be in order at the start of a training session, equipment can break down, and a good training environment will display an internal telephone number where help can be made available immediately.

12   **The layout of training rooms is important.** Formal straight rows of chairs or tables, set out like an examination room, do not provide an environment for a participative training workshop. For effective training, people need both to be comfortable and relaxed, and able to interact easily with each other.

13   **Training can be a vehicle for demonstrating good teaching and learning processes.** A well designed and effectively facilitated training workshop can provide an example of practices and methods which staff can take away from the training event and apply in their own work with students. Sometimes, the techniques used by a good trainer are more memorable (and useful!) than the actual subject content of the training event.

10

Using appraisal to enhance quality

Universities and colleges need to have in place appraisal programmes that link directly to the overall mission, the local plans of the school or department, and the needs of each individual. Appraisal can be a strong positive power when it is used developmentally to ensure that individuals and groups review their own achievements, set realistic goals for the future and think about how what they are doing fits into the whole institutional programme. These tips aim to guide the process away from being a tiresome formality, towards it being an active and dynamic means of coordinating work programmes.

1   **Make sure that the purposes of the appraisal scheme are clear to all staff.** Publish clear guidelines so everyone knows what they should be doing to make appraisal work best for the individual and the organisation. These guidelines should also explain the criteria for allocating resources for staff development, both in terms of time and money.

2   **Establish channels of communication.** Let staff know exactly how to channel information into the appraisal system, and make it clear how this will be used once it is there.

3   **Don't just have an appraisal system on paper.** Run sessions about how the system is intended to work, and include an introduction to the system in induction programmes for all staff. Remember that, however much proof you have on paper that appraisal has been done, if outcomes are never used or followed up, staff will lose confidence in the system.

4   **Feed individual targets into the whole staff development system.** Support staff in setting themselves realistic targets. The line manager can then balance the requirements for resources, and allocate them according to need in a fair and transparent system. If appraisal is not focused on targets, it could merely be a nice friendly chat! Ensure that targets include factors relating to teaching and learning, as well as research.

5   **Train appraisers to undertake their role.** If appraisers have experience of systems elsewhere, they will need to be inducted into the ways of your organisation. Appraisal is often used very differently in industry or other public sector areas, from the way it is used in academic contexts, and it is important that those involved understand the local system. It can be useful to bring an element of fun into training for a serious purpose such as appraisal, and using role-plays can allow people to detach themselves from the process and see it more objectively.

6   **Consider training your appraisees.** This need not be an extensive – or expensive – process, but it will benefit your appraisal system greatly if those being appraised have a clear understanding of what is happening, and what realistic expectations they should have of appraisal. Develop the culture so that appraisees collect, as a matter of routine, evidence they will wish to bring to support them in appraisal. Such evidence can include appropriate collection and analysis of student feedback.

7   **Make appraisal an open system.** This enables individuals to participate, and therefore feel ownership of the policies and processes used by the organisation. This in turn will clearly lead to more cooperation, and thus be more effective.

8   **Improve skills and performance through appraisal.** Use the process to identify ways that individuals can develop themselves and their practices, to enhance the quality of the services which they provide. It is helpful to establish, openly through discussion, clear performance criteria to be aimed for, in every kind of job in the department.

9   **Use the information you gain through appraisal.** If you identify extensive training needs, for example, in the field of information technology, build your institution-wide training programme to meet such needs. If you discover that individual research programmes are ineffective and unfocused, consider ways to bring together researchers into centres of excellence perhaps, thereby achieving a critical mass. A lot of time and energy is invested in gathering the information yielded by appraisal systems, and it is important not to waste this by failing to act on it.

10   **Monitor the effectiveness of appraisal.** Without setting up cumbersome bureaucratic procedures, devise ways in which you can evaluate the strengths and weaknesses of your appraisal system.

11

Managing stress

In order to maintain a high quality working environment for all our staff, ways of managing stress need to be found which can help people cope with difficult times and changing environments. The following suggestions are aimed at helping staff through such periods, both for their own good and for the good of the institution.

1   **Encourage staff to learn to say 'no' (except to you).** Stress is generated by people being asked to do things that are not really their responsibility. Learning to say 'no' to taking on new tasks is really difficult, especially since most people's jobs entail helping people all the time. What staff need to learn to do is to say no firmly, politely, offering alternative suggestions where possible but without apologising.

2   **Help staff to let other people know what they are currently doing.** By making public work schedules or lists of current urgent, medium-term and long-term tasks on the wall for all to see, staff can make their workload explicit and visible to others. When someone then wants to delegate a new task, they can negotiate where it will fit into prioritised schedules and people will (or should) recognise that demands other than their own are being made on people's time and energy.

3   **Enable staff to look after themselves.** Everyone needs to find ways within their jobs and outside it to de-stress themselves, whether it is through exercise, relaxation or gossiping! People who become really stressed are often those who won't talk about how they feel or who try to cope for too long on their own without asking for help. Remind them to take holidays and when necessary to book these in advance, and to fix up things that they will enjoy at weekends.

4   **Set up and encourage support networks.** Making it easier for staff to use gymnasium or sports facilities, for example at lunchtime, can help staff to form support groups. Similarly, interest groups are good for getting staff from different parts of the institution together, and 'togetherness' in all its forms is useful for reducing stress levels.

5   **Create a climate in which staff are realistic about what can be achieved.** Research suggests that people don't get stressed because they have a lot to do, but more because they are worried about whether the time they have available is sufficient to do it in.

6   **Accept that some level of stress is inevitable.** Universities are busy places that have peaks and troughs of workload (peaks mainly!) Attempt to build in flexibility into organisational systems so staff and resources can be targeted to struggling areas where this is possible. Do a stress audit. Find out how stressed staff are in the organisation by asking them, formally and informally. Then act on the information in ways that will help the people concerned and the organisation as a whole.

7   **Avoid a culture in which people are afraid to admit they are stressed.** Staff need to be able to feel free to express feelings about being under strain and should not be embarrassed to seek help when they are not coping. It should not be perceived as a sign of weakness or as an opportunity to put pressure on people to leave the organisation.

8   **Don't boast about how you work late, and only take a third of your holiday!** This only makes other people feel guilty. In any case, overworked people make poor managers, and make unwise decisions. Set an example of reasonable, healthy working.

9   **Recognise that stress occurs at all levels.** People often assume that it is those with the most senior posts who have the most stress at work, but recent research indicates that stress occurs throughout organisations, especially where people bear responsibility but have little power. Investigate ways to defuse stress wherever it occurs.

10   **Bear in mind that stressed staff are expensive.** They make more mistakes, have more time off work and spend energy in unproductive conflict. Resources dedicated to making an organisation as stress-free as possible bear dividends.

11   **Set up a mentoring scheme.** New staff, along with staff newly promoted to additional or different responsibilities need support, especially with adjusting to the lie of the land, and the best ways to try to prioritise their tasks in their new environment.

12   **Managers need to take some responsibility for stress.** Support must be provided for those on whom the institution has laid unreasonable burdens. This might take the form of providing stress management workshops, stress counselling or other kinds of occupational support.

12

Maintaining morale

Complex organisations like universities and colleges are constantly changing. Though there are some people who thrive on coping with change, for most people change causes some stress. The following tips may help institutions maintain the morale of their staff, even in difficult circumstances.

1   **Keep people informed.** Morale can be enormously damaged by half-truths and uncertainties. When it is the case that decisions have not yet been made, it is useful to make this understood by all who may be affected by the decisions.

2   **Have deadlines by which important decisions will be made.** Coping with uncertainty is made easier when people know exactly how long the uncertainty is likely to last. Some decisions need to be made rapidly to address fast-changing external circumstances. However, particularly when making planning decisions about restructuring the operations of staff or departments, it is usually possible to provide some kind of target date, so that people can gear their personal planning into appropriate timescales.

3   **Remind people about all the things that *aren't* changing!** Even when major changes tend to threaten morale, people often get the effects of these changes quite out of perspective. Many of the things they will already be doing will still need to be done in a similar way after changes are implemented. People are rarely required to change more than a small proportion of what they do, in any single period of time.

4   **Keep doors and minds open.** If people are disgruntled, enabling them to have their voices heard is enormously important and can help people feel valued even if they disagree with what is being done.

5. **Collect feedback about people's views on important issues.** This can be done at meetings using 'show of hands' counts, but large meetings take time to set up and arrange, and not everyone can be at them. Short tick-box questionnaires, and telephone questions can also help tap in to the prevailing climate of opinion about issues. The products of such feedback are useful when explaining the position to the vociferous minority (who don't always believe their view is not representative, and may need to see such proof).

6   **Put things into print.** It can be helpful to ensure that all views are well summarised in the minutes of meetings of policy-making committees and boards. This can help people with minority views to see that their views are being taken seriously. Also, policies of recording views can sometimes help people take more care in the ways in which they express their arguments.

7   **Cultivate team approaches to working.** For example, getting a group of colleagues (teaching and non-teaching) to pull together in organising an event such as a conference or an exhibition can improve people's morale, and can be a worthwhile distraction from some of the causes of loss of morale.

8   **Think about awaydays.** These don't have to be expensive. It can be useful to schedule a meeting (whether one of a regular series, or a special event) in an hotel, or at another campus, with transport and refreshments laid on. Just travelling together to and from such a meeting often brings staff closer together in their thinking, and can improve morale.

9   **Recognise that everyone has feelings.** It can often be useful to start a committee or board meeting with a 'what's on top?' round, where everyone is invited to say a single sentence or phrase about what is on their minds at that particular point in time, whether or not it is relevant to the meeting.

10 **Don't forget to celebrate.** Life can become so busy preparing for the next battle that people forget to give due time to celebrating their last triumph. Recognising achievements, and acknowledging people's contributions to them can improve morale and productivity. In a difficult financial climate, it may not be possible to pay staff as well as they deserve. Alternatives which can go a long way include treating the department or section to a meal out, a departmental walk in the country, a pub lunch, a champagne breakfast, a skittles match or a theatre visit. The quality enhancement associated with good team morale is worth such investments.

13

Coping with turbulent times

Many people in universities and colleges agree that these are turbulent times. Some take the first opportunity to escape, maybe taking early retirement where this is an option. However, they often find that it was not so much the turbulence they needed to escape from, but more often the constraints surrounding it. The quality of any institution can be enhanced by the ways staff address such turbulence. The following advice is offered by one whose 'retirement' is much happier – and much more turbulent – than the preceding years!

1   **Encourage a culture where staff keep their 'weather eyes open'.** It can be useful to give everyone the responsibility to monitor news from journals and newspapers – one serious and one fun publication each, and to circulate or post on a notice board news worth being aware of. Turbulence is often associated with unanticipated changes. There are, however, usually plenty of advance signals of likely changes in the policies of governments, funding councils, and professional bodies. It is worth encouraging everyone to spend some time 'crossing bridges', but not too much!

2   **Avoid swimming hard in the wrong direction.** This is in some ways the opposite side of the suggestion made above. While it is worth anticipating changes, it is best not to act decisively or irrevocably until the nature, wisdom and scale of the changes are well known.

3   **Don't ignore the things that don't change.** It can take so much time and energy to respond and react to all the things that do change, that our attention can be distracted from the key purposes of our institutions, and the essential nature of our roles. We must continue to put our students' needs first, and these don't change nearly as fast as politicians' whims.

4   **People don't change much.** Sometimes people get the impression that what is needed is for them to change into entirely different people to cope with changed circumstances. It is more likely that the main requirement may be for people to change some of the things they *do*, and not all of the things they believe in.

5   **Keep things in proportion.** Some things seem to be easy to get completely out of proportion, when changes are about to happen. For example, for some staff, the prospect of being moved out of the office they have inhabited for several years may be seen as a major life change, when in fact many of the things they actually *do* in that place may be done equally well somewhere else.

6   **Don't try to solve everyone's problems.** Work out who actually *owns* each problem. Then work out who may be affected by the problem. Doing this often narrows down the feeling of uncertainty, and helps to establish which problems are most productive to tackle, and which should just be ignored, as the locus of ownership rests elsewhere.

7   **Be supportive to colleagues suffering from stress.** There is a great deal of stress around in higher education nowadays. Help colleagues articulate to you the causes of their stress, as just having someone take time to listen to them often relieves their stress, and the process of explaining it to you often helps them track down the causes of their feelings.

8   **Live for the moment.** Even in difficult times of change, with impending decision deadlines looming, it is possible for small groups of colleagues to plan diversionary tactics. These can include a meal out, a long lunch, a short visit to a local conference (maybe one in the same institution, where there are no costs, and therefore no one to refuse to let you go!) Be creative about satisfying distractions from the turbulence of the day.

9   **Use planners and lists to save you cluttering up your mind.** Find what works for you, for example your diary, a wall chart, a weekly planner, and so on. Making 'to do' lists helps you feel you don't have to remember all of the tasks all of the time.

10   **Don't carry all of your work around with you.** A symptom of overwork and stress is taking home each day far more than you could ever deal with in one evening or weekend. Take home just a small proportion of the mountain, including one urgent job and at least one interesting but non-urgent one. Start on the latter – the former will get done anyway.

11   **Leave your bag or briefcase at work at least one night a week.** You'll have one night when it doesn't gaze accusingly at you all night!

12   **Remind yourself which parts of your work you really enjoy.** Try to increase the proportion of such parts, and while doing these allow yourself to forget the uncertainties and unresolved problems elsewhere in your life. Network with colleagues outside your institution. Benefits that can enhance quality include simply finding out that others have the same problems as you, and sharing solutions and strategies.

Chapter 3 Enhancing Learning Through Teaching And Assessment

The quality of the learning outcomes and learning experiences of our students is a primary concern of all staff in our institutions, and this chapter aims to offer practical suggestions about straightforward and effective ways about addressing and enhancing this quality.

We start with 'Student learning support'. One of the most important outcomes of higher education should be that our students emerge from our systems as better learners, more self-sufficient and confident, and ready to continue to learn throughout their careers. It can be argued that the subject-specific curriculum is the vehicle through which this more important development should occur. Especially now that the student population is considerably more diverse than it used to be, addressing students' needs for help in becoming better at learning is paramount. We offer suggestions about how to embrace this need on an institutional level.

Next we consider the effects of the learning environment on students' educational growth. Enhancing the quality of the learning environment not only promotes better learning, but helps staff and students alike to feel more valued, overlapping with the needs addressed in the first two chapters. In addition, suggestions on improving the quality of the learning environment lead to the sort of visible evidence of quality that will not fail to be noticed by quality assessors/reviewers.

Next, we turn our attention to the curriculum. We start with some suggestions about enhancing the role of well expressed and well chosen learning outcomes. Learning outcomes have received considerable attention in many institutions, but are not yet always fully utilised to help students gain a clear picture of what is required of them. We give two sets of suggestions about one particular dimension of the curriculum: student projects. We start with some general points which should help student projects play a realistic and useful part in their learning experience, then give more specific advice on ways of ensuring that such projects are seen as purposeful in our strategy of developing a variety of life skills in our students. All of our suggestions here have been made bearing in mind the questions that teaching quality assessors/reviewers are briefed to ask about student project work.

In many subjects, laboratory work plays a major part in the overall learning experience of students, but it is not always clear to students exactly how this work fits in to the overall picture of their courses, or how much it counts for in their overall awards.

Discussion of this is followed by suggestions aimed at enhancing student learning in small groups. Ideas about varying the processes used in small-group work with students are aimed at helping both staff and students enhance the quality of the learning that students derive from working in groups.

Next we suggest ways of enhancing the quality of learning in large groups, in particular in the lecture situation. (A more detailed discussion of lectures and large-group learning is in Chapter 6 'Preparing for Quality Assessment Visits'.)

We end this chapter with two sets of suggestions about assessment. It can be argued that assessing our students is the most important thing we do for them, as the qualifications that result from our assessments influence their whole careers and lives. Moreover, it is increasingly recognised that the ways that students approach their learning are profoundly influenced by the nature of the assessment processes and instruments they are preparing to meet. Our advice on enhancing the quality of assessment should be seen as the basis for a charter of assessment principles, and an agenda for improving the contribution of assessment to learning. Our final set of suggestions is on diversifying assessment, and we offer some starting points for considering a number of assessment processes over and above those traditionally used in higher education. This discussion should only be seen as an introduction, however, and we would refer readers who wish to go into much more depth regarding the details of a wide range of assessment techniques to our earlier volume, *500 Tips on Assessment* in the same series as this book.

14

Student learning support

With a much higher proportion of people engaged in further and higher education than was the case some years ago, it is to be expected that more students need help regarding the most effective ways of learning. The following questions should help colleagues to check out whether student learning support is likely to be keeping up with demand. We have written the questions in the context of students 'belonging' to a department or a course, so you will need to address the rather more complex issues involved when students are undertaking modular programmes and do not 'belong' to anywhere in particular; it is then even more important that there is some learning support provision which all students are aware of and can actually use.

1   **Is there timetabled learning skills development provided in your department?** Subject-specific learning skills support is one of the most effective ways of ensuring that students benefit from advice and suggestions which relate directly to their studies, rather than general advice, only some of which may be useful.

2   **Is there college-wide provision of learning skills support?** Timetabled study skills sessions are provided in many institutions, necessarily focusing on general aspects such as time management, task management, revision strategies and exam techniques. Are details of such provisions communicated to your students? It is important to give particular attention to support and guidance during the first part of the academic year, not only to help students who discover problems as they enter higher education for the first time, but also to establish the presence of the support mechanisms and personnel.

3   **Is one-to-one support available in your department?** Personal tutor systems can accommodate an individual student's particular needs regarding learning support. Alternatively, some departments provide a subject-related learning support counselling service, usually arranged by one or two members of staff with particular expertise in helping students with study problems.

4   **Is general one-to-one support available in the institution?** Student counselling services often cater for students from any department or discipline with general learning problems. Do students in your department know of such opportunities which may be available to them?

5   **Is there good liaison between your department and the student support services?** It helps a great deal when members of teaching staff know the staff of student support services, and are aware of the kinds of support that are available to students.

6   **Is learning support visible and available even before interview?** Some students will know of specific needs or problems, such as dyslexia, and being able to discuss such needs at the earliest opportunity can do much to allay anxieties students may have.

7   **Is special support available in the library?** For example, students who are visually impaired may not be able to read signs or seek information. Good liaison with support services can help to ensure that library staff are prepared to help.

8   **Have you considered providing online learning support?** Computer mediated conferencing (CMC) may be suitable for general study skills support across an institution and for course-specific support. Such technologies can help to make the best use of the time and skills of staff who can provide learning support help. Using such support online is the ideal scenario, with help available very quickly, but it can still be useful if help replies can be provided within a day or so of requests being made by students using e-mail.

9   **Are you making good use of the intersemester break?** Where there is such a gap in teaching provision, it can be the ideal time to offer students study skills workshops, as well as training in the use of computers, media facilities, and IT provision.

10   **Is appropriate learning support available to students learning in non-traditional ways?** For example students on distance learning, flexible learning, or resource-based learning pathways or independent-study elements of courses may need additional, focused help on how to go about organising their studies independently and effectively.

11   **Is there appropriate staff development?** As the student population becomes more diverse, teaching staff need to become better at helping their students to learn effectively. It is important that staff development does not only cover subject-specific issues or teaching methodologies, but also that it addresses student learning styles.

12   **Is there good networking of staff across the institution regarding learning support?** It is useful to have a group or committee meeting two or three times a year to bring together those members of departments who take particular responsibilities for ensuring that students learn effectively.

13   **Is good practice in learning support disseminated across the institution?** One way of spotlighting and spreading good practice is to hold an annual 'Good practice' day focusing each year on an aspect of effective learning. It is useful to have this sort of event opened or chaired by someone very senior, to give messages to all that learning is at least as important as teaching or research.

15

Learning environment quality

The quality of students' learning – and indeed of our teaching – is related to the quality of the learning environment. A good learning environment helps students to feel valued. Alternatively, a stark cold room with serried rows of desks can instil fear and trepidation, and bring back bad memories of exams (think back!) The following suggestions may help you improve conditions for teaching and learning.

1   **Value the importance of a high-quality learning environment.** We have all experienced teaching in less-than-adequate learning environments. However, it may be useful for you to remind yourself what it feels like to be a student in the rooms you use; sit down for a few moments where they sit and see how it feels.

2   **Get an overall picture of the current situation.** Walk round your campus, and in particular the buildings you work in, role-playing the view of visitors or new students. Check that someone is responsible for collecting the information upon which improvements and developments can be based and coordinated.

3   **Work with, not against, those responsible for accommodation.** Being in charge of room allocations tends to be a thankless and difficult task. Get to know who has this function in your institution overall, and in your school or department. Such people can do more with constructive positive suggestions than with grumbles.

4   **Allocate resources sensibly.** Resources are scarce, but it is important to earmark your share of them on an annual basis, and continually make visible improvements to the quality of the learning environment. Consider forming a committee with clear terms of reference and responsibilities, and with sensible representation from academic, technical and administrative staff. Such a committee may only need to meet two or three times a year, but can still make major contributions to planning and prioritising.

5   **Decide priorities.** A brainstorming session with colleagues can lead to sensible decisions about how best to use limited funds and resources to enhance the quality of the learning environment. One approach is to agree minimum standards for classrooms, lecture theatres and laboratories, and to identify where the most serious deficiencies are.

6   **Plan short, medium and long term.** It is important to have available at all times something more robust than a wish list. Sometimes, a limited amount of funding may become available at short notice, to be used immediately, and it is important not to resort to whims when deciding how to use it.

7   **Build up a strategic plan.** Major changes to resource allocation need to be part of whole-institution decisions. You have more chance of making a strong bid for resources if you are seen to have thought carefully through your needs, and decided the best way to make use of those resources.

8   **Consider setting up specific responsibilities.** For example, appoint a member of staff to keep an eye on things in one room, including clearing out outdated material from notice boards, removing and sorting through piles of discarded handout materials lurking in corners, noticing and doing something about items such as clocks or audio-visual materials that are not working, and so on. It is equally useful to allocate specific responsibilities for areas such as corridors and lobbies.

9   **Cherish your technical staff!** They are extremely valuable, not least when it comes to maintaining and improving the learning environment. Encourage members of your technical staff to adopt roles as 'carers' for particular rooms and teaching areas, and involve them in deciding the minimum levels of equipment needed, and the optimum provision that may be hoped for some day. Also involve them in planning how best to handle equipment breakdowns, and whom to approach for help in such instances.

10   **Involve students.** They are on the receiving end, and know what works, and what doesn't. Solutions to problems are not always expensive, and students are more tolerant when they understand the problems and constraints, and feel their views are being taken seriously.

11   **Evaluate your success.** Continual monitoring and updating of the quality of your learning environment is necessary. For example, when a teaching area has been refurbished, select some classes and arrange an evaluation. Be sure that this is supported by the lecturer whose time is used for gathering student feedback. A prize of a £10 book token goes a long way towards convincing students that their feedback is being sought seriously. Be sure to let both staff and students know the results of the evaluation.

16

Quality of learning outcomes

Over the last two decades there has been a steady progression towards expressing the intended learning outcomes of each course, module and unit of study, rather than just giving a syllabus as a list of the topics to be taught. Essentially, learning outcomes are statements of exactly what students are expected to be able to do when they have completed given elements of their studies. They are suitably expressed objectives or aims of each part of a course or module, usually supported by descriptions of the sorts of evidence that students should become able to furnish in due course to demonstrate their achievement of the objectives. Quality assessors/reviewers (and more importantly, staff and students themselves) can find well-expressed learning outcomes a good indicator of the scope and depth of any programme of study. The following suggestions may help your programmes to be seen to be good.

1   **Collect examples of ways that other people express learning outcomes.** For example, look for learning outcomes close to your own field as expressed in other universities, and in Open University modules. You may often find that other people have already done much of the work in converting a list of topics into well-explained learning outcomes, which you can adapt or adopt in your own course.

2   **Make sure that learning outcomes are known to the students, and understood by them.** Too often, time and care has been taken writing and expressing learning outcomes, which then are filed in syllabus or validation documents, rather than being put to use with the students to help them know exactly what they are expected to become able to achieve.

3   **Ensure that learning outcomes are sensible.** There should always be a good answer to any student's question 'Why do I need to become able to do this?' It can be worthwhile to write down a short sentence of justification for the inclusion of each and every learning outcome; this helps decide which outcomes can sensibly be ditched!

4   **Make the learning outcomes clear.** It is best to avoid statements such as 'Students will be able to understand the Second Law of Thermodynamics'. It is better to express such an outcome in terms of the things they will be able to *show* for that understanding when they have achieved it.

5   **Use language that is accessible to everyone.** Avoid the temptation to try to make learning outcomes look impressive by expressing them in sophisticated language. As far as possible, keep jargon terminology out of learning outcomes, so that they can be understood by students who have not yet studied the subject, and by colleagues who are not specialists in it.

6   **Don't write your learning outcomes entirely on your own.** It is really useful to compose learning outcomes with other people who are doing the same thing. You can then ask each other 'What does this one *mean*?' and write down good answers to this question as better statements of the learning outcome in discussion. Group drafting and editing is always more effective, and leads to learning outcomes being understood not only across each course team, but by the students.

7   **Don't write too many learning outcomes.** One of the dangers of trying to express syllabus content in terms of learning outcomes is that it is dangerously easy for the some of the outcomes to be trivial ones, even when they are things that students are required to be able to do.

8   **Don't be too prescriptive.** Rather than spell out learning outcomes in an attempt to describe everything that students should become able to do, it is worth keeping some of the outcomes more generic, and illustrating them with a 'for example' rider, rather than spelling out all the possibilities. This allows you to bring in more 'for examples…' as you think of them as you work with students.

9   **Look for gaps.** When anyone appraising the quality of a course looks at the content as expressed in terms of learning outcomes, it is important that nothing crucial can be seen to be missing. Ask other people 'Is there anything important that isn't covered here yet?' as you draft learning outcomes. Check that the learning outcomes cover an appropriate range of skills, maybe using taxonomies such as Bloom's to ascertain whether all the things that should be addressed by each element of curriculum are represented.

10 **Think of the evidence which will indicate achievement of the learning outcomes.** Many competence-based frameworks already combine statements of intended learning outcomes with descriptions of the sorts of evidence that learners are intended to produce to demonstrate their achievement of the outcomes. 'Performance indicators' and 'range statements' can be useful to give extra detail (to students, as well as to quality assessors/reviewers) of the level of the intended outcomes.

11 **Don't concentrate on learning outcomes to the exclusion of learning processes.** The processes dimension gives the added value to learning outcomes. Paying increased attention to the processes increases the probability of the learning outcomes being achieved in ways that are flexible and transferable.

12 **Don't be put off the learning outcomes approach by all the bad examples that are around!** The fact that many published outcomes-based schemes are in existence, where the outcomes are badly phrased, or simplistic, or ambiguous, does not mean that the approach is an ineffective one.

13 **Put the learning outcomes to use.** Don't leave them fossilising in the course validation documentation or the student handbook. Tell students which outcomes they are working towards in each lecture, tutorial and assignment. The learning outcomes are devised for the benefit of students, and need to be made to work well as part of how they find out exactly what they should be trying to achieve. Make sure that students know when they have achieved learning outcomes, and can recognise them as things they have added to their range of skills, and can build on them. It is also useful to explain to employers about the use of learning outcomes, illustrating them with relevant examples, and listening to suggestions that employers may offer about additional things that could be included as learning outcomes.

17

Enhancing student projects

Student project work is often the place where the higher levels of learning are involved, and such work is often of crucial importance in establishing students final award classifications. Some of the suggestions below are based on the sorts of features that teaching quality assessors/reviewers are briefed to look for when they investigate the effectiveness of student project work.

1   **Make sure that the goals of project work are clearly identified.** The intended learning outcomes of student project work are often the most ambitious goals of a syllabus, and it makes the syllabus look all the more credible and worthy if these goals are transparent. Involve the students themselves in identifying targets, specifying evidence, and working out criteria by which the products of their project work can be judged.

2   **Make sure that project work is oriented towards higher level intellectual skills.** Project work can be the ideal vehicle for developing skills of analysis, synthesis, critical thinking and so on. Think, for example, of the difference that could be expected between a sixth-form project and final-year undergraduate project on 'renewable energy sources'.

3   **Give students some room to negotiate the work to be undertaken and the ways in which it will be assessed.** Because of the individual nature of student projects, it is appropriate that students are given a degree of flexibility and choice in the way they develop their work and exercise their higher level skills.

4   **Ensure that the learning outcomes associated with projects are clearly understood by students.** Because of the individual nature of most student projects, the general goals expressed in the syllabus may have to be translated into specific targets in the context of each project.

5   **Structure project work well.** Because of the nature of project work, it needs to be broken down into manageable chunks to help students not to flounder due to the enormity of their perception of the whole task. Having

a 'project plan' as an assessed part of the overall product, and doing this element of assessment at an early stage, helps to ensure that students themselves structure the overall task in sensible phases.

6 **Check that project work is clearly documented in the student handbook.** Where student projects not only take a substantial proportion of students' time on a course, but also carry great significance in their final assessments, it is logical that the nature and scale of the related documentation and guidance for students should reflect the importance of the project work.

7 **Work out stage deadlines for each project.** Where each student project is different, the nature and timing of the deadlines will need to be handled individually, and preferably will involve negotiation with the students involved. Clear deadlines not only help students keep to task, they also alert you to students who may be in danger of becoming casualties in their project work.

8 **Provide help for students with time management and task management.** One of the objectives of project work is to help students to develop such skills, but project work is too important for students to do this by trial and error. Written guidance materials may be useful, but it is better to couple these with one or two group sessions where students can confront and address the process issues involved in projects together.

9 **Be explicit about the assessment criteria for project work.** Teaching quality assessors/reviewers regard the assessment criteria as one of the best ways to see exactly what is being covered by student project work. Students themselves are better able to perform well when they have a clear idea of what is going to be measured.

10 **Ensure that project supervision is continuing and supportive.** Some students will need (or want) more support than others. It is important to be able to demonstrate that supervision was at least adequate, not least in the event of student appeals against assessment decisions where project work did not succeed.

11 **Build up a collection of evidence of past students' project outcomes.** A library of good (and bad) examples can help students gain a sense of perspective regarding the quality and scope of the work expected of them. Get students to examine such evidence, for example by asking them to identify three major skills which each piece of evidence demonstrates.

12 **Try to avoid some students doing far too much project work.** The danger is that such students may spend too much time on projects at the expense of other parts of their overall programme of study, and may (for example) succeed brilliantly with the project, but fail an important exam.

18

Making student projects purposeful

We have already explored some of the contextual and support issues around the quality enhancement of student projects. The following suggestions are based on ensuring that the purposes and justification of project work are evident to students, colleagues and anyone else examining the quality of student project work. Most of the purposes listed here are developed from suggestions offered to teaching quality assessors/reviewers regarding what they should look for in project work.

1 **Use projects to help students explore important topics more deeply.** The more extensive timescales of projects can allow students to go further into topics than they could otherwise do in class situations, particularly in modularised, semesterised systems where time may be at a premium.

2 **Whenever possible, make projects real.** Remain on the lookout for clients or sponsors, or for ways of including in project work responsibilities for the students themselves to identify clients or sponsors.

3 **Set projects which help students apply their theoretical knowledge to practical problems.** Project work can allow students to apply a much broader cross-section of the theory they have studied, than can shorter assignments. Projects therefore serve as integrating and linking devices, helping students to see the connections between different parts of their learning

4 **Design projects to train students in research skills.** Many of the more successful students are likely to proceed to lengthier episodes of research, and project work can help them find out what this will feel like, and whet their appetites. Project work can also help such students to discover by practical experience many of the most important do's and don'ts regarding good practice in research.

5 **Use project work for students to demonstrate initiative.** Project work is one of the best ways of recognising and accrediting student initiative. It is much harder to make appropriate allowance for initiative in many other parts of any syllabus, where assessment criteria need to be formulated in advance and matched to predetermined learning outcomes.

6 **Help project work to develop independent thinking.** In many parts of a course it could be argued that a tendency towards convergence of thinking is intended or inevitable. Project work allows for a move away from this, as it encourages students to take an increased level of choice and control over the themes, processes and outcomes of their projects.

7 **Use project work to develop appropriate team skills.** Many projects involve at least some cooperative or collaborative working. Especially when working with large groups of students, it can be useful to design project work so that for part of the time students are intended to work in groups, and then go on to follow up individual strands on their own.

8 **Help students to be aware of the other skills they are developing.** While doing project work, students necessarily develop time management skills, keeping-to-task skills, coping strategies, leadership skills and self-reliance. Project supervisors can help students to recognise these other skills, and develop them more consciously. Better still, integrate these skills as an intrinsic part of the course.

9 **Establish the agenda of developing written communication skills.** Writing up project work involves similar written communication skills to those needed in research or writing formal reports for employers. Project supervisors can help to train students in these skills, by giving them regular feedback during project work, as well as at the end of the projects.

10 **Use projects to alert students to different target audiences for their written work.** Writing a full report or dissertation may not always be the most useful target (not least because the assessment of such products takes so much time). Alternatives can usefully include a draft journal article, a magazine article aimed at a non-specialist audience, or a funding proposal for further work on the basis of the project findings.

11 **Include oral presentation skills in the agenda.** Students are often required to give a short presentation to a group of their peers (and a tutor) after completion of their project work. It can be particularly beneficial to bring in some peer assessment of such presentations, not least because this helps students to learn much more from each other's approaches.

19

Enhancing laboratory work

In some subjects, important learning outcomes are associated with practical work in laboratories. Such outcomes can include practical skills which may be essential in the subject concerned. The following suggestions may help to ensure that the quality of students' learning experience in laboratories is enhanced.

1   **Ensure that each practical activity has clear, worthwhile purposes.** It is important that there are convincing answers to any student who may ask 'Why exactly am I required to do this?'

2   **Provide clear explanations of the intended learning outcomes of each practical activity.** The objectives of individual experiments are often highly specific, and can be based on the acquisition of practical competences or relate to interpretation of data and the links between theory and practice. Alerting students to all objectives is a first step towards helping them demonstrate achievement.

3   **Do students have the opportunity to prepare specifically for each laboratory class?** When students have already done some preparation, the quality of their learning experience in the laboratory is greatly enhanced. Issuing laboratory scripts, for example one week in advance, and requiring students to complete some preliminary questions about the particular practical work *before* they come to the laboratory, can have substantial dividends regarding the learning payoff of the practical work.

4   **Check that printed instructions for the use of instruments and equipment are clear and apposite.** Students could be given their own copies of such details in advance as part of their briefing for the sessions, but it can be useful to ensure that a durable, step-by-step version of the instructions (a laminated poster) is displayed on site in the laboratory.

5   **Ensure that students have good support in the laboratory.** Support is often provided by demonstrators or postgraduate research students. Such staff may benefit from training in how to help students learn-by-doing, rather than merely being on hand to deal with questions or problems.

6   **Have you done the experiments you have designed for your students?** This question may seem a strange one, but as practical work develops and changes it is often the case that lecturers or supervisors may not have actually performed some of the operations that their students are required to do in the laboratory. Having done at least the main steps in a piece of practical work puts you in a much better position to help students learn to do it, and anyone supervising or demonstrating in a laboratory should aim to have this experience to draw on.

7   **Consider how students are being observed in the laboratory.** If their actual practical competences are to be assessed, it is not enough just to base this assessment on their final practical reports. It can be useful to bring in demonstrators to give some assessment of the practical skills of students when this can be carried out fairly and objectively.

8   **Observe how students' time is spent in the laboratory.** For example, is there any unnecessary queuing for particular pieces of equipment, and if so, can the experiments be scheduled in such a way as to minimise this? Are students kept waiting for demonstrators or supervisors to explain particular stages of the practical work to them? Are students left at a loose end for significant periods while experiments proceed, and are there useful and interesting things they could do instead during such times?

9   **Is there any possibility of passengers?** With large classes, when groupwork is necessary in a laboratory, it is important to ensure that all students are involved fairly in the practical work. Task allocation briefings and appropriate observation can help to ensure this.

10   **What is being assessed?** Ensure that the same things are not being assessed time and time again. For example, skills involved in writing full practical reports are important, but are sometimes over-assessed (taking a lot of staff time). Briefing students to produce short-form reports for some of the practical work is a solution. Structured report formats can be used for some experiments, with students entering data directly into a workbook or a computer program. It is usually much more important that students *interpret* and *analyse* their laboratory findings than to write up experimental procedures in full every time.

11   **Consider getting students to submit 'instant reports' before leaving the laboratory.** When their work is such that they tend to be finishing experimental work and leaving at different times, this can be done without too much queuing. You can then give them feedback comments on these 'quick' reports before they leave, and maybe reduce the proportion of experiments to be written up in full after they have left the laboratory.

20

Learning in small groups

Tutorials, seminars, and other small-group situations can be highly productive learning experiences for students. Larger class sizes make it more difficult to provide such occasions for students, and it is therefore important that the quality of those sessions which are provided is as high as we can make it. The following suggestions provide some do's and don'ts which can enhance the quality of students' learning in small groups.

1 **Make sure that the goals of each tutorial are clearly communicated to students.** Sometimes the goals can be published in advance, while on other occasions the goals will depend on the questions and issues that the students bring to the occasion. In either case, the learning payoff is enhanced if the goals are established or reviewed at the start of the session concerned.

2 **Help students to know the purposes of small-group work.** Students often don't really know what the differences are between the different kinds of teaching–learning sessions on their timetables, in terms of the different sorts of behaviour expected of them, and the teaching-learning processes involved in each kind of small-group work. The more students know about *why* we are giving them small-group work, the better they can benefit from such occasions.

3 **Prepare for small-group sessions.** There is a tendency (as noticed by teaching quality assessors!) for tutors to prepare well for lectures but not for tutorials. This leads students to come to their own conclusions about the relative importance of each of these teaching–learning environments.

4 **Don't talk too much!** A problem with small-group sessions is that it is all too easy for the tutor to fill all of the available time. Even when answering students' questions, it is usually more productive to provide good short answers to several questions than an in-depth definitive answer to just one question.

5   **Make good use of question-and-answer processes.** Come in to a small-group session with a list of questions you may or may not actually ask, and concentrate first on all the questions you can draw from the students. Towards the end of a tutorial, you can select from your 'unanswered' questions some for the students to prepare their own answers ready for a future session. It can be useful to give each member of the group a different question to go away with (but make sure that none of the questions are so difficult that the students will not return on the next occasion).

6   **Ensure that student participation is high on the agenda.** Getting *all* the students to participate is quite an art. Just asking for verbal contributions can allow the confident, pushy student to dominate. Asking each of the students to write down their own immediate answers to a question, for example on post-its or small pieces of overhead film, can be a way of promoting equal participation opportunity, and can help the more retiring students provide their contributions to the group. Vary the nature of students' activities, for example getting them to make flip chart lists, post-it replies to questions, mind-maps, pictorial metaphors, flow charts, and so on.

7   **Think about introducing student-managed small-group sessions.** These can be occasions where the students themselves are given freedom to prepare the content, and manage the processes by which they tackle the topic concerned.

8   **Don't ask questions that just depend on recall.** It is much more useful to consider questions which help students to make sense of what they are learning than just to remind them about what they may have forgotten.

9   **Don't ask too many questions at once.** Learning in small groups happens best when the students know exactly which question or issue they are addressing at a given time. It can, however, be useful to write up the 'whole' list of questions on a flip chart, so students can see where each question fits into the whole picture.

10   **Don't put a student on the spot with a difficult question too early.** This can deter students from participation, and can even make them so uncomfortable that they may choose not to attend your next session with them. It is much more acceptable to put some of the students on the spot with hard questions towards the end of the session, but move away from them if they have not got ready answers, as these questions can then be the agenda for the next session, giving all the students involved some time to prepare their answers.

11 **Don't ask questions then answer them yourself.** Though it can be hard to wait for students to work towards the answer to a question, and you may be itching to provide the answer, students will learn a lot more by struggling if necessary. You can help them converge towards a good answer by giving feedback on those parts of their thinking that are along the lines required, and explaining to them why other ideas are not correct or appropriate.

12 **Don't ignore students' answers.** Even when students give incorrect or confused answers to a question you've asked them, they need some helpful feedback on *their* answers, and not just to be told what the right answers should have been. Where possible, build on students' own responses when leading towards the correct answers.

21

Ringing the changes in groupwork

There are many different ways of enhancing the quality of learning in student groups. The following suggestions expand on the question-and-answer ideas for use in tutorial-type sessions given elsewhere in this book, and are among the processes which teaching quality assessors are looking for in their observations of groupwork.

1   **Get individual students to prepare and present seminars.** This can include the student leading the seminar, taking questions from the rest of the group, and maybe also from the tutor involved. The attention of the student audience can be significantly increased by getting the students receiving the seminar to use processes of peer assessment, with straightforward and well-expressed criteria which have preferably been formulated by the student group.

2   **Consider getting pairs or groups of students to prepare and present seminars.** This can be less intimidating than solo performances, and can involve the development of useful cooperation and collaboration skills. Again, peer assessment can help *all* the students involved get more from such seminars.

3   **Use tutorless groups for appropriate learning activities.** These give students the freedom to contribute without the fear of being found lacking, or making mistakes in front of a tutor. For such groups to work well, it is useful to provide the students with carefully formulated briefings in print, and to require an appropriate report-back product. This helps the students keep on task.

4   **Use buzz-groups in large group sessions.** These are particularly useful for generating in an informal way a lot of ideas or opinions, which can then be reported back and explored in greater depth with the large group.

5   **Use brainstorming techniques to generate ideas.** This is useful in small groups, and still works well with groups of 20 or more students. It is important to formulate strict ground rules for brainstorming, such as 'give no comment on ideas already given', 'say "pass" if you've nothing to add when it's your turn', and 'think creatively and say anything that comes to mind'. After producing as many ideas as possible in a few minutes, the group can start prioritising and clustering them.

6   **Use snowballing or pyramiding to refine ideas.** This can be a way of enhancing learning in quite large groups by getting students to work together in a structured way. For example, get students to think of ideas in pairs, then combine with another pair to take the ideas further, and then combine with another four to prepare a report-back to the whole class.

7   **Use crossovers to enhance students' communication in groups.** For example, divide a group of 16 into four groups of four. Set the small groups a first stage task, then ask one member from each group to move to another group and report the findings. Set the second stage of the task to the revised groups, then ask a different member to move on and report, and continue doing this till everyone has worked with everyone else.

8   **Consider using fishbowls in medium-sized groups.** For example, from a group of 20 students, six could be drawn (or volunteer) to sit in a circle in the middle of the room. The inner circle could then be briefed to discuss a scenario, with everyone else observing, and with an exchange mechanism by which students from outside the group wanting to make contributions could replace someone in the group.

9   **Use role-plays to help students contribute more easily.** Some students who are reluctant to contribute to group discussions or debates because of shyness, lose most of such inhibition if they are playing someone else. Printed handout sheets giving sufficient details of each role help students to adopt the role they are intended to play, and are useful for allowing each student to react to the other roles involved as they unfold in the role-play.

10 **Self-help groups can enhance students' learning.** It can be worthwhile to start such groups up with tutor support, and help the students in each group start out to generate their own ground rules and targets. Then the groups can be left to operate without further support, other than perhaps a mechanism to bring unresolved problems to a class meeting or to a tutor.

22

Enhancing large-group teaching

One of the most visible activities in higher education tends to be large group teaching. Teaching quality assessors / reviewers look carefully at what happens in large groups. You may remember some guaranteed ways of ensuring that students are bored, including reading lectures aloud, failing to make eye contact, speaking in a monotone, too much hesitation, disorganisation, or having nothing interesting to add to conventional textbooks. The following suggestions for improving students' experience in such situations are based on the points such assessors are briefed to look out for during their observations of teaching.

1   **Reconsider the purposes of large-group sessions.** Now that information technology, resource-based learning and autonomous learning are features of higher education, think of ways of making the best uses of lecturers in large-group sessions, such as to stimulate, enthuse, illustrate, 'make real', and answer questions from students.

2   **Make the most of the venue.** Many large-group sessions are scheduled in non-ideal venues, but even then lecturers can often make the learning environment better, for example by making best use of the lighting, checking that screens or markerboards are as visible as possible, helping students to choose seats where their sightlines are unobstructed, and using microphones or other audiovisual facilities to their best advantage.

3   **Ensure that students can see where the content fits into the whole course.** Simply spending a little time establishing the links between the present lecture and previous ones can help students to gain a sense of perspective. It is also useful to keep reminding students about the links between the lecture content and the main study resources they are intended to be using.

4   **Check that each lecture has a clear structure, and that this is explained at the outset.** Expressing at the start the intended learning outcomes for the lecture helps students to be more receptive about the main parts of the content. Using a little time towards the end of the session to remind students of the outcomes consolidates what they have gained from the session, and helps them to add useful summaries to their notes.

5   **Watch for signs that students are following what is being said.** The body language of students gives some indication regarding whether they are understanding the lecture, but it is much more useful to make the lecture interactive by asking students questions, to gauge whether they are following the lecture well.

6   **The quality of handout materials is a measure of the effectiveness of large-group teaching.** Teaching quality assessors/reviewers look carefully at handouts, and will look at how well they help students to get to grips with the topics of lectures. Interactive handouts that involve students in practising and problem-solving are examples of good practice. Desktop published handouts can look much more credible than photocopied handwritten notes!

7   **Audiovisual aids should enhance learning.** It is worth working out exactly what students should learn from each instance of the use of such aids, and explaining to students why the aid is being used, and what they should do with the information they see and hear.

8   **Audibility is important.** This is not just a matter of voice projection to the furthest parts of the room, but is also about appropriate speed of talking, and making sure that students are not having any difficulty in hearing clearly.

9   **Timing needs to be appropriate.** Time management in large-group sessions is an important part of a professional approach to teaching, and a lecture should end in plenty of time for students to move to and from the lecture-room ready for the next session.

10   **Enthusiasm is one of the key factors students link to the quality of lecturers' teaching.** It is hard to tell anyone how to demonstrate enthusiasm, but everyone knows this quality when they see it!

11   **Highlighting and summarising are important.** Students often need all the help we can give them to work out what the key points are in a subject that is new to them.

12   **Brief students carefully regarding follow-up work.** Students benefit from suggestions about how to flesh out their notes, how to structure their reading, where to find examples, which problems to try for themselves, and so on. Lecturers often grumble that students don't do enough work between lectures, but the reason is sometimes that students can't work out what they should be trying to do.

13   **The nature and extent of the interaction that a lecturer promotes in large groups is probably the most important indicator of learning quality.** This includes asking students questions, answering their questions, but more importantly, getting students interacting with each other as part of the session.

23

Enhancing the quality of assessment

Assessment is the most important thing that happens to students, as the results of assessment not only influence their careers and lives, but the design and timing of assessment are major factors predetermining the ways they structure their learning. The evidence accompanying assessment instruments and processes is everywhere, and is a major area for investigation by quality assessors/reviewers.

1   **Staff should have training relating to assessment.** Without adequate training and practice, new staff should not be authorised to set or mark any assignments or exams which count towards students' overall awards. Experienced staff should continue to be monitored in those aspects of their work relating to assessment.

2   **It is essential that part-time staff should be aware of assessment practices and regulations.** They almost inevitably will contribute to students' assessment, and sometimes they are left to their own devices in this, with no real training, monitoring or support.

3   **It is vitally important that assessment practices are revisited regularly.** There is a tendency for assessment to be seen as an add-on to the task of helping students to learn, and this leads to staff being too complacent about assessment. The fact that 'it's always been done this way' is no guarantee that it is the best way, or even that it is working effectively.

4   **Assessment should be seen to be valid.** In other words, we need to ensure that each form of assessment that is used is measuring what it is intended to measure, and that it is closely related to the expressed learning outcomes which students are aiming to achieve.

5   **Assessment should be consistent, fair and reliable.** In particular, it is important to take every possible step to remove as much as possible of the subjectivity which can lead to unfair assessment. Clearly expressed assessment criteria, carefully formulated marking schemes, and processes such as double-marking can all contribute visibly to the campaign against unreliable assessment.

6   **Assessment should be transparent.** It is necessary to remove the hidden agendas which so often seem to be involved in assessment. Students need to know what the standards and requirements are, and processes and instruments of assessment need to be open to inspection by everyone involved. Bringing in employers or practitioners as contributors to assessment can ensure that assessment is more closely related to real-world perspectives.

7   **Assessment should be appropriate in amount.** Many people now believe that over-assessment is a major problem in higher education. It is probably more important to improve the quality of assessment, even when this may mean reducing the quantity. It is just as important that assessment workloads are realistic and acceptable for students as for their assessors.

8   **Assessment should provide students with as much feedback as possible.** Students do not learn much merely from exam marks or assignment grades, and can learn much more from feedback about things they did well and things they did badly. Using students as peer assessors can help to ensure that they get more feedback than is possible just from academic staff, and peer assessing helps students to develop critical and analytical skills.

9   **Assessment processes should promote learning, not just measure what has been learned.** The use of self-assessment and peer assessment can both help learners make more sense of what they have been learning, and derive more feedback than they may get from other forms of assessment. Assessment tasks need to include challenging and stretching components, rather than just demonstration of recall capability or practised competence.

10   **Students should be involved in formulating at least some of the assessment criteria.** Getting students to work out suitable criteria to use, for example, in peer assessment of some of their essays, reports, presentations and so on can be a valuable way of helping students to think more deeply about the subjects involved. Also, when students have a sense of ownership of the criteria to be used in assessment, they go to greater lengths to demonstrate that they can meet these criteria.

11   **Care should be evident regarding the timing of assessments.** For example, learning is damaged when several assignments are set in different modules for the same students with deadlines too close together. Also, sufficient time needs to be allowed between the time when the last material in a module is covered and the related assessment, so that students have adequate opportunity to master the material.

12   **Assessment regulations should be well designed, clearly expressed, and known well by students and staff alike.** For example, clear differentiations need to be shared between staff and students about the difference between plagiarism and due acknowledgement of sources.

13   **A workable appeals system needs to be in use.** When for any reason students are not satisfied that justice has been done regarding their assessment, an efficient and open re-examination or moderation system should be available to reassure them or to rectify any unfairness found.

24

Diversifying assessment

Every form of assessment disadvantages the students who are least skilled at handling it, and it is important not to disadvantage the same students all the time by using only a narrow range of assessment formats. Increasing the variety and range of assessment processes and instruments can play a major part in enhancing the quality of assessment, and the contribution of assessment to effective learning. The following suggestions may help increase the variety and interest of assessment, and lead to increased feedback to students.

1   **Examinations need not be restricted to unseen written ones.** Other forms of exams which can be more closely linked to measuring students' true achievement of learning outcomes can include short-answer and structured-question papers, open-book exams, exams without time constraint, and case-study-based exams.

2   **Written coursework assessments can take many forms.** Alternatives to assessing essays and reports can include assessing short essay-plans, annotated bibliographies, pieces written in the form of magazine articles, short-form reports, research article drafts, funding proposals, critical incident accounts, and abstracts.

3   **Oral exams can be reliable.** When a standard, well-designed interview checklist is used as the basis for oral exams, they can be as fair as any other kind of exams, and test verbal communication as well as knowledge or understanding.

4   **The assessment of seminar presentations can be accompanied by high learning payoff.** Students put a lot into their preparation for such seminars, and well-facilitated usage of peer assessment can provide them with useful peer feedback which deepens their learning.

5   **It can be useful to get students to do assessed presentations to people from outside the institution.** Panels drawn from industry or the professions can be discerning judges of student presentations, and can be very constructive in helping to design the assessment criteria relating to such presentations.

6   **Plans and drafts can be worth assessing.** Assessing early attempts at essays or reports can give students useful feedback, with opportunities to learn from this to redeem mistakes or misconceptions.

7   **Portfolios can provide an accurate profile of students.** Though portfolios are time-consuming to assess well, they can contain collections of evidence reflecting a wide and diverse range of students' competences, and can allow different students to excel in their own individual ways.

8   **Poster displays can provide a useful alternative medium for students to show their understanding and individuality.** When coupled with peer assessment, such displays also help students to learn a great deal from each others' approaches.

9   **Self-assessment can be coupled with other forms of assessment.** For example, asking students to write a short self-assessment of some work they are handing in for tutor assessment causes them to reflect on their work, and deepen their learning. Such self-assessments also alert tutors to those students who have an unrealistic belief in the level of their own learning, though the majority of self-assessments turn out to be very realistic in practice.

10   **Computer-based assessment can be very reliable and can provide full and rapid feedback.** When well-piloted structured questions are turned into computer-based assessment programmes, students can work through such programmes on their own or in exam rooms, with the computer doing the scoring and also displaying or printing out feedback messages relating to each entry made, or option chosen by students.

11   **The products and processes of student groupwork can be assessed.** Groupwork promotes cooperative and collaborative learning, and develops teamwork and leadership skills which are valued by employers. While it is normally fairly straightforward to assess the products of groupwork (which can take the forms of reports, presentations, and so on) it is also necessary to use ways of probing and assessing the relative contributions of each student to the final product, and combinations of self-assessment, peer assessment and tutor assessment may be appropriate for this.

Chapter 4   Quality Processes

One reason we have left this chapter till now is that we wanted to give practical help to colleagues first to enable them to start thinking about ways to adjust or develop their practices directly linked to their everyday work with students. We therefore begin this chapter by stepping back from the teaching–learning–assessment interfaces to look at systems. Quality systems are examined by assessors, and others making judgements on the performance of our institutions, and our suggestions are focused on ways of keeping these systems under review.

Record-keeping could be regarded as part of the systems in our educational institutions, but is a matter which is close to the everyday work of staff. We offer practical guidance on things to remember when addressing the everyday task of keeping records on students' progress and achievements.

Equal opportunities is rightly on the agenda of all who inspect or judge our institutions. It is one thing to have an institutional policy on equal opportunities, and another to extend that policy to the everyday working of everyone in the institution. Our suggestions may help towards the latter.

We next address some of the processes of committee work in our institutions. Committees are the bane in the lives of many colleagues in universities and colleges, but are nonetheless essential parts of an effective institutional setting. Our extended list of suggestions, therefore, is aimed at enhancing the quality of committee work to make it more effective, efficient and focused.

We end this chapter with two sets of suggestions about external examining, which is seen as a major plank in the structure of quality assurance and the guaranteeing of standards. This plank is also an exposed one, as the quality of our teaching and assessment is seen by people from outside our institutions, and the processes are open to inspection by quality assessors/reviewers and funding agencies. We begin by offering advice on how to go about choosing external examiners in the first place, before moving on to a more detailed analysis of the ways that they can play useful parts in the overall picture of quality enhancement.

25

Reviewing systems

Any large organisation depends on having procedures and practices which underpin all kinds of aspects of its overall operation. However, there is the danger that systems can remain in place long after their original purposes have changed or even disappeared. The following suggestions may help you review the quality of your systems, and fine-tune them to enhance the quality of your institution.

1   **Build in review cycles for *all* systems.** It is worth having a definite review date for each system, and a planned meeting when its use will be discussed or revised. It is better – and faster – to review regularly all systems whether they need changing or not, than to carry on implementing outdated systems due to 'lack of time to review them'.

2   **Don't change for the sake of change.** Some systems may be working perfectly adequately, and the benefits achieved by changing them may not match up to the time and expense of implementing the changes. Don't assume that because it's an old system it must need changing. Look at fitness for purpose – and make sure the purpose is still important.

3   **Be on the lookout for duplication of effort between systems.** It can be worthwhile adapting one system to be able to handle the data collected for another purpose, rather than implementing an additional process to collect similar data.

4   **Consider the sort of reviews that *don't* serve useful purposes.** Many review exercises turn out to be well intentioned, well documented, but end up as paper-producing exercises ('feel the thickness') or number-crunching exercises (it is too easy to just turn data into statistics). Such exercises rarely end up telling us what we need to know, and too often are ways of hiding what we don't want to know!

5   **Consider bringing in someone with systems expertise.** A skilled consultant may be able to suggest time-saving processes which will quickly pay for the expense involved in obtaining such advice. Word-of-mouth is the best recommendation, so ask around about whose advice proved useful in other organisations or institutions.

6   **Go back to the rationale for each and every system.** Ask why it was introduced in the first place, whose purposes it serves, and how important it is in the overall structure and operation of your institution. If the purposes have changed, or the processes are no longer the most sensible ones to deliver the required results, the system is ripe for review.

7   **People like their own systems!** While to the administrative mind it may make sense to have uniform systems across a whole large institution, the individuals involved in schools and departments may have a strong sense of ownership of individual systems they devised, and which work well for them. Intelligent creative people can ensure that a system they don't like will be seen to fail, and fail definitively!

8   **Distinguish between mission and practice.** There is usually more than one way of ensuring that a system upholds and strengthens the mission of an institution or department, and different practices which work need to be accommodated. It may be essential that the *products* of the systems are compatible, but the processes may remain individual to local areas of an institution.

9   **Review the strengths and weaknesses of each system.** It is tempting to concentrate on what is going wrong when reviewing systems, but it remains important to give credit for the things that are running well. A new, better system is usually one which builds on the strengths of a previous incarnation, rather than one which 'rubbishes' everything that happened previously.

10 **Plan carefully when making major changes to a system.** It is sometimes worth carrying on with the old system in parallel with the new, until it is quite certain that the new system is workable and reliable.

11 **Review your systems reviews!** Like any other change, it is important to evaluate objectively the effects of changing or developing systems. Feedback needs to be collected and analysed not only from those involved in the new processes, but also those whose work or studying may be affected by the new system. Three years seems a useful cycle for renewal: one year getting it right, the second year doing it really well, and the third year slipping a little towards being routine. Without review, by the fourth year things can be institutionalised, and lacking their own sense of purpose.

26

Record-keeping

It is easy to complain that there is far too much paperwork around, but the problem is often not so much the quantity as the quality of the paper mountain. The following suggestions may help to reduce the time wasted on record-keeping activities, while at the same time increasing the value and relevance of the records that are kept.

1   **Make sure everyone is aware of the records they are required to keep.** For example, assessment regulations may require all coursework assessments and exam scripts to be kept, along with the results, for a named period of time, sometimes as long as five years.

2   **Be aware of the legal situation regarding records on computer.** Staff and students have the right to inspect any data about them that is stored electronically. This means it can be worth thinking twice before storing data of a sensitive nature.

3   **Allocate responsibilities for data storage.** Problems often happen when it is not certain who holds responsibility for collecting, storing or analysing records. Clearly designated job descriptions help to avoid this sort of problem.

4   **Encourage staff to 'get filed properly'!** An experienced administrator can spend a few hours 'filing' a lecturer's paperwork, and setting up a system which is straightforward to maintain and will save countless hours in the future. Systems that work efficiently in large offices can be extended and adapted for an individual's needs and requirements. Hard-pressed lecturers will not, or cannot, find the time to make such systems for themselves.

5   **Don't have a record-keeping system that is totally dependent on the person who holds overall responsibility for it.** It is important that other people can take over at short notice when the normal keeper of a particular variety of records is away or unavailable.

6   **Think carefully about what records are worth keeping.** What purposes will the information serve? How is it best to arrange the records to lend themselves to anticipated uses? Keeping records just because they have always been kept is not a good enough reason for the time, trouble and expense that may be involved.

7   **Do an audit of the uses to which existing records are put.** This may not only give indications of records not worth keeping, but also lead to insights into the most appropriate formats for keeping the records.

8   **Consider an archive for old records.** For example, when collections of records have served their purpose but are seldom needed any longer, it can be better to arrange their temporary storage in some low-value space, maybe at a site where space is not at a premium.

9   **Be prepared to destroy old records.** Collections of data often only get destroyed when key personnel move away or retire, or when a major institutional change or disaster occurs! It can be worthwhile to obtain advice from an experienced archivist, when deciding what should not be kept any longer.

10 **Keep important records in secure ways.** It can be worth storing crucial records (including assessment data) in more than one format, and at more than one location. This obviates the disasters that could occur in the event of a fire or flood, for example.

27

Practising equal opportunities

Ten tips cannot possibly cover the scope of ensuring good practice in equal opportunities within universities and colleges, but a book about enhancing quality would be deficient if it didn't touch on the area. Remember that the agenda of equal opportunities can include issues of race, gender, special needs, disability, dyslexia and many other dimensions. Here are a few ideas which could help to build an agenda for equal opportunities:

1   **Ensure there is an equal opportunities statement of principle.** Some universities are shocked to discover they have nowhere codified their position on equal opportunities. Such a statement, however imperfect, at least provides a starting point for good practice.

2   **Explore good practice elsewhere.** Many institutions have in existence excellent documentation and systems for equal opportunities. These can be scrutinised, evaluated, amended and borrowed from, in order to set up or improve a university's own practice.

3   **Collect data for monitoring.** Most universities keep good statistics for students on balance of gender, race, disability and so on, but some don't. Few universities can be fully confident that they are really well informed with data on their staff or even their students. Without sound data, it is impossible to know whether an employer is employing disproportionate numbers of particular groups in particular sectors, and this could lead to accusations of inequality of treatment.

4   **Involve people.** Equal opportunities practice should include at a decision-making level the categories of people who are involved. For example, an equal opportunities committee, which contained no black, disabled, female, mature or junior members would hardly be credible. Equal opportunities policy practice should be participatively designed and implemented, rather than based on top-down decisions.

5   **Discuss different dimensions of inequality.** Institutions need to be aware of equal opportunities dimensions associated with ethnicity, religion, gender, disability, age and sexual orientation. Frequently institutions can boast a good record on one or two of these areas, complacently ignoring others.

6   **Principles alone are not enough.** Institutions need to monitor how effectively principles are being turned into practice, and to collect examples of evidence to justify their claims to be equal opportunity employers.

7   **Set goals and targets for improvement.** If an institution recognises that it is unrepresentative in its employment patterns or has areas of unequal practice built into its structure, it is not easy to rectify these overnight. Nevertheless, it is possible without tokenism to set achievable goals for improvement within specific deadlines. It is as well to be cautious about quotas or positive discrimination, however, as there can be legal implications for these.

8   **Be aware of legislation.** Universities and colleges need to be fully aware of equal opportunities legislation in terms of services they supply and employment they offer. Not only is it good practice in an institution seeking to enhance quality to ensure equal opportunities practice, it can also ensure the avoidance of costly litigation, and the costs of adverse publicity.

9   **Think about equal opportunities and your franchisees.** Can you be sure that the institutions to which your courses are franchised practise equal opportunities policies at least as good as your own? If not, you may wish to explore how best to ensure that they do, or build suitable criteria into the conditions underpinning franchise arrangements.

10 **Promote commitment to equal opportunities.** Ensure that equal opportunities practice in your institution is not just a paper exercise, but one which is integral to practice. It is impossible to ensure that every member of staff and every student subscribes to and complies with your policy, but it is important to carry as many hearts with you as you can.

28

Enhancing the quality of committees

A considerable amount of time can be spent by academic and non-teaching staff preparing for, attending, and following up the business covered in committee meetings. It is therefore very important that their time is used to the best. The following suggestions may be useful both to those involved in committee meetings, and those servicing committees or planning the ways that committees function at both departmental and institutional level.

1   **Include 'effective committee participation' in induction and staff development programmes.** This can help to ensure that future committee participants are suitably trained, and that staff who take on important committee roles have opportunities to develop and practise some of the key skills they will need.

2   **Ensure that the agendas are carefully constructed.** For example, split the agenda into parts, such as 'Agenda A' items that are the ones for discussion, and 'Agenda B' items for information only.

3   **Sequence agenda items in order of importance.** This helps to ensure that the key items are placed early and discussed while members are feeling alert, and also therefore helps to ensure that meetings get off to a punctual start. Leaving important items until ten minutes before lunch is not likely to ensure the best outcomes.

4   **Institute a policy where agenda papers are sent out two weeks before each meeting.** This gives members more opportunity to read the papers, and allows them time to gather additional information which they may need to be able to contribute to the meeting.

5 **Have set start times and finish times for meetings.** This helps everyone plan their time efficiently, in particular by avoiding people running late because of earlier meetings which overran, and can restrict discussions to sensible lengths of time.

6 **Put a time limit against key agenda items.** This may need some careful planning before the meeting, but can help to ensure that key items are given appropriately balanced amounts of time. It also gives people an indication of how much time can be given to individuals' contributions to the discussion of each item.

7 **A well-prepared Chair is the key to good meetings.** The Chair needs to be well briefed for every item on the agenda, and also needs to ensure that the papers sent out before the meeting give people as much information as they need to prepare for the discussions. The Chair needs also to ensure that appropriate information is tabled during the meeting, but only when it would not have been possible for it to have been available in advance. A good Chair also plays a key part in helping to keep meetings professional, and avoiding members becoming fraught or emotional. When tempers are becoming frayed, it can help to encourage other members to participate. Summarising the opposing points of view can help give members time to regain their composure. A spontaneous 'comfort break' is another device that can help soothe agitated members.

8 **It is important that meetings are kept to time.** A Chair who is a good timekeeper helps to ensure the smooth running of the meeting, and needs to be firm with any members who prolong discussion, for example by thanking them for their contributions, then moving the meeting on to another agenda item.

9 **It is useful to have ground rules such as that the Chair will summarise at the end of every agenda item.** This is a useful way of closing the discussion of items which otherwise may go on too long, and helps members to be clear about the outcomes or decisions reached by the committee, and also helps the secretary take appropriate notes for minutes.

10 **All members of committees should be encouraged to participate.** Some members will be naturally quiet and not as forthcoming as others. However, one of the roles of a good Chair is to enable every member to contribute. This can be done by being firm with dominant members and asking quieter individuals for their views.

11   **It is useful to spread who leads agenda items.** If the Chair presents every item, meetings can become tedious. Involving others, but with careful control of the time allocated to the items, can help to result in full and active participation by all members, and lead to greater productivity of debates as members take ownership of the various topics.

12   **Consider a policy of sending out the minutes within two weeks of the meeting.** The minutes should be structured to remind members of the outcomes and decisions. When members' names are listed beside action points, they are reminded about the matters they were allocated to follow up, and having the minutes published quickly gives them more time to do this properly.

13   **Not only the Chair should be well prepared for a meeting.** All members have a responsibility to be well prepared, as this leads to more informed and effective debates.

14   **Minutes should be structured so that decisions and action points are boldly labelled.** When actions are required before the next meeting, it helps if both the nominated persons' names, and the specific actions required, stand out clearly from the minutes. For example, action points may be placed in the right-hand margin, or typed in bold at the end of the minute of each agenda item. It should be possible to ascertain by a quick scan of the minutes, who is responsible for what actions, and by when. It can be useful for the Chair or secretary to issue separately timely reminders to members whose actions will be the basis of key discussions and decisions at a forthcoming meeting.

15   **Minute secretaries should be well trained.** Minuting a meeting is not an easy task. Many institutions provide training courses, sometimes through Staff Development Units. Appropriate staff should be encouraged or required to participate in such training, even if they are quite senior personnel in the institution. This enables a climate of effective minuting to be established in an institution, with comparable methods and standards across schools or departments.

16   **Meeting rooms should be prepared in advance.** The right tone is set for a meeting when members walk into a room that has already been set out with the agenda papers and other appropriate information, and it can be useful to print out and arrange name plates or cards where members may not already know everyone. This particularly helps new members tune in to the workings of a committee.

17   **Table layout is important.** Long narrow tables do not help promote discussion, and people may strain to hear what is happening. Where possible, a round or oval table shape allows everyone to see and hear each other effectively, and encourages everyone to participate.

18   **It is useful to have committee meetings evaluated.** A properly trained evaluator, working round a series of committees in the institution, can play a key role in formulating recommendations for policies for promoting the effectiveness and efficiency of meetings. Such an evaluator can, for example, check to what extent the desired outcomes have been achieved at meetings, and offer constructive comments for the improvement of meetings. It can be useful to appoint such an evaluator each year, enabling others to gain this kind of experience, and bringing a 'fresh eye' to the processes.

19   **Refreshments are not unimportant!** A three-hour meeting without any drinks can lead to dry discussions! It can be appropriate to have drinks waiting on arrival (and this can also help to ensure a punctual start!). For long meetings, further refreshments will be needed, and it is worth timetabling a definite refreshment break into the agenda. Such a break need not be long, as the meeting can resume with members having their coffees or teas at their places, but the fact that there is a break can be useful for members who may need to make an urgent phone call.

20   **Colour-coded documentation can enhance the effectiveness of committee papers.** Paperwork supporting main agenda items photocopied on different coloured papers can be helpful. It can be easier for the Chair to refer to a particular set of papers by colour. It can be useful to adopt a running theme of colours for matters that span several meetings of a committee, as this can help members file the correspondence.

21   **Minutes need to be effectively filed.** While it may be up to the individual members how they file their own copies of the minutes, it is very helpful if all committee minutes are systematically and accessibly filed, in date order, in key locations in an institution. This can be a great help in processes such as internal or external audits.

29

Choosing external examiners

External examiners are widely seen as playing a crucial part in quality assurance, and when well chosen and used effectively, can also play key roles in quality enhancement. The time will come when there will be some sort of register of approved external examiners, but for the present much depends on choosing the most suitable people without such a quality backup. First, we look at some of the factors to be taken into account in selecting the most appropriate people for the role.

1 **Develop your own network of potential external examiners.** Going to conferences, participating in local and national networks and committees, and following up contacts in other institutions, are all ways of assembling a pool of people from which to choose suitable external examiners.

2 **Avoid compromising choices.** A widely held criticism of the way external examining works (or fails to work) is based on situations where there is at least a hint of an 'old colleagues network' (usually described in more sexist terms!) at work. In other words, don't choose your friends (but that does not mean that you must remain unfriendly to your external examiners).

3 **Don't think too local.** An external examiner from another institution too close to home may not be thought of as being sufficiently detached and impartial, especially if on some levels the institutions are competing.

4 **Don't think too distant.** While choosing an external examiner from a considerable distance gets over some of the problems of directly competing institutions, the prospect of being an external examiner is less attractive if two days are going to be spent on travel for each visit. Also, long journeys can mean expensive travel claims.

5   **Choose on the basis of experience as well as on subject expertise.** The most helpful external examiners tend to be those who are experienced in examining as well as being sufficiently expert in the topics involved. They can then bring to your course their experience of how external examining works (or doesn't work!) in other institutions. However, every external examiner has to start somewhere, so look out for situations where it is sensible to bring someone new on board, for example as a second examiner, allowing them to gain experience from someone else as they work for your course.

6   **Get external examiners to the institution before appointing them.** It is very useful to arrange a visit for a potential external examiner before official duties are involved. This sort of informal visit can be really productive in helping the external examiner to get to know quite a lot about the staff and students on the courses to be examined, and also allows the staff teaching the course to get to know the external examiner before formal roles set in.

7   **Make sure you can make a good case for the appointment.** In most institutions, appointments of external examiner have to be approved by an appropriate committee, sometimes at a senior level, and it's worth sparing yourself (and your nominee) the considerable embarrassment which accompanies a suggested external examiner being rejected.

8   **Make sure the person concerned wants to do the job!** External examiners are not at all well paid in most cases, and in some cases all payments go to their home institution. To have enough motivation to do the job well, they need to have better reasons than the small fee or awayday involved.

9   **Decide what you expect of your external examiner.** It is useful if potential examiners are given an accurate picture of their intended role before they are offered an appointment. This can spare you – and them – the troubles that occur when the role is unclear, and a mismatch develops between their view of their role and yours.

10 **Be prepared for a change in the relationship between you, and your external examiner.** People you thought you knew quite well in informal relationships at conferences and networks can behave differently from your expectations when charged with the duty of being positive but critical influences in the development of your course.

11 **Try to arrange a rollover period.** When one external examiner is going to take over from a previous one, it can be very useful if they serve together for one year, and attend the same meetings. This helps build continuity in the ways that the role is developed.

30

The role of external examiners

External examiners can serve many roles. It's worth deciding the combination of roles you intend your externals to serve before drawing up the terms of their appointments. It is also worth leaving yourself sufficient freedom to adapt or extend their contributions to the quality enhancement of your course.

1   **External examiners can validate standards.** Most institutions ask external examiners to comment on the relative performance of students compared to those on similar courses elsewhere. Remember that not all external examiners should cite student performance as being 'above average' in such contexts!

2   **External examiners need to be demonstrably impartial.** It is not acceptable just to send them the work of those students that you think they should see (for example borderline cases, or the best of the bunch!). Discerning external examiners ask to select randomly from the class list the names of the students whose work they require to examine, in addition to any problem cases you wish to place before them.

3   **External examiners don't just examine – they report.** Most institutions take external examiners' reports seriously. Some institutions ask each and every external examiner questions, as part of their contract of appointment, which enquire well beyond the standards of the students on the course. Such questions address, for example, the conduct of the assessment of the course, and the effectiveness of the communications between the course team and the examiner.

4   **External examiners sometimes act as members of course teams.** To do this at a distance, they need to be informed as a matter of routine of decisions made by the course team, and aspirations for the future development and quality enhancement of the course.

5   **External examiners can be sources of informal advice.** When changes or developments are planned, it can be well worth asking for the views of external examiners.

6   **External examiners may be able to help with validation procedures.** In fact, external examiners are sometimes chosen from outside people brought in to help to validate a new course. Serving external examiners may well be able to help with re-validation of the course, or at least may be able to provide recommendations for changes and developments as a course evolves.

7   **External examiners need to be taken notice of.** When suggestions or recommendations are included in external examiners' reports, most institutions as part of their quality assurance provision, monitor in one way or another whether the recommendations are being acted upon, or addressed appropriately.

8   **External examiners have to avoid compromising situations.** For example, it is not ethical to invite an external examiner to undertake some paid consultancy work that has any bearing on the course to be examined, or it could be argued that impartiality could be jeopardised. It is not, however, unethical to combine a visit by an external examiner with some other paid activity totally unrelated to the course examined.

9   **Remember that external examiners are busy people.** Their diaries need to have your Assessment Board dates, for example, up to a year ahead of the event. And don't expect them to be able to turn round some candidates' work within a week of posting it to them. Arrange such matters carefully with them beforehand.

10   **It's hard to get rid of external examiners!** They normally serve for a fixed term of three to five years, and can be safely dispensed with when their time is completed, but if there is a major disagreement between an external examiner and a course team (or course leader), this has to be lived with until such time comes. If the disagreement becomes public, most of the blame is likely to be attributed to the course team (or leader) rather than to the examiner.

Chapter 5   Feedback And Evaluation

One of the most significant areas where data can be gathered to fuel the processes of quality enhancement is through feedback from the principal client group of our educational institutions: the students. Student feedback also serves as evidence to those charged with assessing or validating the quality of the teaching, learning and assessment processes that students experience. Furthermore, student feedback can often be used as visible evidence of at least one part of the quest for quality enhancement – that of knowing where it is most important to begin enhancing. More importantly, student feedback evidence can show conclusively that efforts to enhance particular aspects of quality have indeed been successful.

We start this short but important chapter with some suggestions about questionnaires. Feedback from questionnaires is relatively easy to obtain, and can be straightforward to analyse, but too often the actual data that questionnaires yield is much less useful than it could have been, not least due to asking the wrong questions in the first place. Also, students get more than fed up when asked repeatedly to fill in the same kind of questionnaires time and time again, and the usefulness of the data that can be extracted from their responses under such conditions is very doubtful. Our suggestions, therefore, are about devising questionnaires which minimise the dangers mentioned above, and ensuring that the information collected is important rather than routine. We offer suggestions about the design of both structured questionnaires to collect the sorts of information that these lend themselves to best, and open feedback questionnaires to probe more deeply into students' feelings and experiences.

Next we consider some of the ways in which feedback can be gathered from students using interviews. 'If only we had the time...' you might be thinking. However, in a genuine quest to formulate the best agenda for quality enhancement, interviewing students can deliver a depth of feedback which exceeds the best that can be done through questionnaires. When student interviews are devised in ways already making use of all the feedback that may have already been gathered through questionnaires, the interviews become much more productive and cost effective.

We continue by offering some broader suggestions about 'Establishing a culture of student feedback', not least to ensure that feedback is properly analysed and used, and that students are kept fully informed of the principal matters arising from their feedback, and the ways in which it is planned to address these matters.

We end this section on student feedback with some suggestions on how to make best use of the feedback that can be derived from student representatives on course committees. At its worst, such representation can fail to deliver any tangible benefits, and may be seen as a token gesture to democracy. When, however, student representatives feel valued for their contributions, the value of their contributions increases commensurately.

31

Designing structured feedback questionnaires

Feedback questionnaires often play a major role in researching the kinds of information which may be needed to plan quality enhancement developments. The following suggestions may help you work out how best to use questionnaires to lead to quality enhancement. Though a good questionnaire is often a mixture of structured and open-ended questions, we'll explore each separately, and you can choose your own balance accordingly. We begin with structured questionnaires, including tick-boxes, rating scales, prioritisation questions, and so on.

1   **Structured questionnaires can have the advantage of anonymity.** Even if using a mixed questionnaire containing open-ended questions as well, you may decide to issue the structured and open-ended parts separately because of this factor.

2   **Don't make questionnaires too long!** Students – and anyone else involved – get bored if they have long questionnaires to complete, and the decisions or comments they make become 'surface' rather than considered ones. Even though students may be able to respond to a structured questionnaire of several pages in relatively few minutes, the fact that a questionnaire *looks* long can induce surface response behaviour.

3   **Consider the visual appearance of your questionnaires.** Go for a varied layout, with plenty of white space, so that it does not look like a solid list of questions. Use a mixture of response formats, such as deletions or selections from lists of options, yes/no choices, tick-boxes, graduated scales, and so on – make it *look* interesting to complete.

4   **For every part of the questionnaire, have definite purposes, including positive ones.** Don't ask anything that could prove to be superfluous or of passing interest only. Ask about positive experiences as well as searching for weaknesses.

5 **Plan your evaluation report before you design your feedback questionnaire.** It helps a great deal if you know exactly how you plan to collate and use the responses you will get from your questionnaires. Working out the things you hope to include in your report often alerts you to additional questions you may need to include, and to superfluous questions which would not actually generate any information of practical use to you.

6 **Make each question simple and unambiguous.** If students' interpretations of the questions vary, the results of a survey are not valid enough to warrant statistical analysis of any sort. In particular, it is worth ensuring that in structured questions, students are only required to make decisions involving a single factor.

7 **Ask yourself 'What does this question really mean?'** Sometimes, your reply to yourself will contain wording which will work better in your questionnaire than the original idea you started with.

8 **Avoid safe middle ground in scales.** For example, the scale 'strongly agree, agree, undecided, disagree, strongly disagree' may give better results if the 'undecided' option is omitted, forcing respondents to make a decision one way or the other (or to write 'can't tell' on the questionnaire, which then has the validity of a conscious decision).

9 **Be aware that some respondents will make choices on the basis of those they think they are expected to make.** Many respondents set out to please the person gathering the feedback, maybe thinking of possible recriminations if critical selections are traced back to their authors.

10 **Keep prioritising questions short and simple.** For example, if students are asked to rank seven factors in order of value (or importance), it may be easy enough to analyse the best and worst choices, but difficult to make a meaningful analysis of the middle ground.

11 **Pilot your draft questionnaire.** There is no better way to improve a structured questionnaire than to find out what students actually do with it!

12 **Feed back the results to your respondents.** Tell them about the changes that are proposed on the basis of the results from the questionnaire. Otherwise people are likely to become disillusioned about the whole process of giving feedback.

32

Designing open feedback questionnaires

As mentioned in the previous section, most good questionnaires use a balance of structured and open-ended questions. The suggestions below may help you get the most from students' responses to open ended questions in questionnaires.

1 **Include some questions that aren't too open!** For example, when seeking feedback about the most successful and least successful features of a course, make your forthcoming evaluation of students' responses simpler by making each question relate to particular aspects of the course.

2 **Remember that students' responses can be influenced by their mood at the moment of answering the question.** Ideally, you may wish to balance this source of variation out in one way or another, for example by issuing a similar questionnaire at another time, and comparing responses, or by including some alternative questions in other parts of your questionnaire which test the same agenda so you can be alerted to inconsistency in responses due to swings of mood.

3 **Don't leave big spaces for students to fill in their replies.** You can compensate for this restriction later with 'Any other comments?' space. If students responses are necessarily short, you are more likely to get easily interpreted answers to your questions, which helps make statistical analysis more fruitful.

4 **Decide whether you want the questionnaire to be anonymous, optional or respondent-known.** With responses involving handwriting, there is always the possibility of tracing respondents, and students may respond differently with this possibility in mind. With computer-based open-ended questionnaires, this dimension is simplified, but not entirely overcome if log-in data could be used to trace respondents.

5 **Resist pressures to over-use standard questionnaires.** This applies equally to structured or open-ended versions or mixed-mode questionnaires. Students quickly get bored with identical questionnaires, and are likely to fall into a standard mode of response, where there is considerable 'echo effect' carried forward from previous decisions and responses. The most useful feedback data is normally generated by specially produced questionnaires relating to a specific course or subject, or a particular aspect of the teaching and learning in that subject.

6 **Try to get a good response rate.** When questionnaires are filled in during contact time, you are more likely to get everyone's views. If questionnaires are taken away by students to be sent back later, there is a tendency to get lower response rates, and the students who actually go to the trouble of responding may not be representative of the whole group.

7 **Give students some free-ranging questions.** For example, it's worth considering asking them 'What other questions should be included in future editions of this questionnaire?' and inviting them to supply their own answers to the questions they think of. Such data is unsuitable for any statistical purposes, but is valuable in qualitative analysis of feedback from students, and can often touch on aspects that relate to potential quality enhancement developments.

8 **If doing a survey by post, supply a stamped, addressed envelope.** This is a significant psychological persuader in encouraging people to respond to questionnaires. It is a way of indicating that responses are indeed valued. Even where internal mail facilities can be used, an addressed reply envelope helps in this respect.

9 **Work out how you are going to analyse the data from open-ended questions.** Sometimes a transcript collecting all responses to a question is necessary before the gist of the feedback can be discerned accurately. In other circumstances, counting the number of times something is mentioned in students' responses can be a valuable process.

10 **Don't accumulate piles of uninterpreted questionnaire data.** It's best to make a deliberate effort to produce a summary report (even if only for your own private use) for each set of data. A pile of feedback responses quickly becomes out of date as new developments are implemented in courses. Also, it is worth helping students to see that it is worth their while to provide feedback data, and showing them that you take the data seriously enough to analyse it straight away.

33

Feedback from interviews with students

Interviews with students can be a valuable source of feedback, and a rich source of ideas for quality enhancement. However, interviewing students is costly in terms of time and effort; the following suggestions may help you to make it a cost-effective process.

1   **Prepare your agenda carefully.** To enable you to analyse and collate the feedback you get from students, it is important that they are all asked the same questions in the same way. It is all too tempting to develop the agenda on the basis of the replies of the first few students, so it is usually worth piloting your question list on a few students (not necessarily from the group to be targeted) before starting on a set of real interviews.

2   **Link interviews with other means of getting feedback from students.** If you are already using (or planning to use) structured or open-ended questionnaires, you may find it worthwhile to work out what else you will be particularly looking for in feedback from interviews.

3   **Consider the merits of using interviews to follow-up questionnaire feedback.** When you have already analysed questionnaire responses by students, you may be able to pinpoint a few issues where you want to ask students more detailed or more personal questions about their experiences with a subject or a course.

4   **Consider the alternative possibility of using preliminary interviews to establish the agenda for feedback questionnaires.** This would probably not take the form of interviews with the whole group, but with a representative selection of students.

5   **You might not be able to interview the whole group.** Decide how you are going to select the students you choose to interview. There are many possibilities, each with its own advantages and drawbacks. For example, you could select randomly by name or student number, or you could make a representative selection including high performers, middle-range performers and low achievers in related assessments, or you could ask for volunteers (not, however, the most representative of the possibilities).

6   **Remember that students could be anxious.** Any kind of interview might make students feel as if there is an assessment dimension present, and this could cause them to be restrained, especially when it comes to expressing dissatisfaction.

7   **Ask questions which lead students to answer rather than to refrain from comment.** For example, asking students 'Was there anything you found unsatisfactory?' could be less fruitful than asking 'What was the thing you liked least about the way this module was taught?'

8   **Don't lead your witnesses!** It is one thing to ensure that students feel free to answer questions, but another to lead them towards the answers you want, or the answers they might think you want. 'Do you like the way I used coloured overheads in my lectures?' is an obvious example of a leading question.

9   **Consider interviewing groups of students.** Students might be more forthcoming in a group, and you could consider posing the questions (maybe as a handout), leaving the group to come to decisions about how they wish to answer them, then return to hear their answers. Students have the safety of being able to report minority views or controversial views, without the student who actually speaks such responses having to own the view reported. Group interviews can actually save a considerable amount of time compared to solo interviews, and allow students to compare and contrast their own perspectives. Students in groups can also be helped to prioritise or sequence in order of importance their responses, making their feedback even more valuable. Group interviews can also be used to get students to clarify or explain issues or responses which at first might be unclear.

10 **Make good notes.** After four or five interviews, you will have a good idea of the general nature of responses to your questions, but you could have lost a lot of the specific detail. More recent interview happenings tend to drown earlier ones in the memory.

34

Establishing a culture of student feedback

'Not another questionnaire' we often hear students groan! With the fragmentation produced by modularisation and semesterisation, there is the danger that students become snowed under by a plethora of separate questionnaires on each and every aspect of their experience. The following suggestions may help the right balance to be achieved.

1   **Plan an institutional strategy for student feedback.** This does not mean that there should be uniformity in every department; appropriate feedback devices may be very different in programmes as diverse or distinctive as humanities and engineering. However, an institutional strategy does mean that someone has thought about the overall implications of the various possible options.

2   **Obtain the big picture first.** It is dangerously easy for feedback to be collected about the nuts and bolts, but not about the whole engine. The questions should be asked 'For what overall purposes are we seeking student feedback?' and 'How do we intend to use the overall data?'

3   **Undertake an audit of current feedback practice.** In our increasingly busy institutions, it is often difficult to know what someone is doing in the next office. Finding out what is happening at local and institutional level can help to clarify thinking, and be the basis for disseminating best practice.

4   **Build student feedback strategies into quality assurance procedures.** This helps to ensure that matters arising from student feedback can be picked up at management level, and addressed appropriately.

5   **Involve staff in the design of student feedback processes and instruments.** Members of staff may have employed successfully their own feedback mechanisms for many years, and it is important to value their experience, and avoid replacing something that was going well with something less effective.

6   **Involve students in discussions about a culture for gathering and addressing their feedback.** Students know what works for them, and what causes them problems. Sometimes staff may not be aware of the big picture problems, while students can be very good at suggesting ways to identify and quantify such issues.

7   **Work closely with the Students' Union.** Officers of the union have a wealth of experience of working with, and listening to students. Joint meetings about feedback processes and instruments can help to focus on important issues, and can lead to union encouragement to students to participate fully in giving feedback.

8   **Variety is the spice of life!** Each of the many methods available for collecting student feedback has its advantages and disadvantages. Using a variety of methods can help to ensure that a much fuller picture is obtained, and that students don't become irritated by the monotony of giving the same sorts of feedback again and again.

9   **Close the feedback quality loop.** Students want to know what has happened as a result of their comments, and the reasons for any decisions which result. Create ways of reporting back to staff and students changes which are being implemented as a result of feedback.

10 **Evaluate your institution's feedback systems.** It is useful to triangulate information about how well feedback is working, by comparing findings about it from teaching staff, students, and support staff.

11 **Don't forget the good points!** It is very easy to focus actions on the negative feedback which may be gathered, and the 'could do better' agendas. The 'well done' agenda is just as important, and it helps to recognise and celebrate those responsible for positive feedback, and build on such strengths.

35

Feedback from student representatives on course committees

Most institutions have policies on student representation on decision-making committees and boards. Student feedback gathered this way is often seen as a major factor in gathering quality enhancement data. Student representation is, however, not without its problems. The following suggestions may help you to make the most of having student reps on committees.

1   **Try to ensure that the right person is chosen to represent student views.** Too often, the duty is thrust upon the first student who shows interest – or who is too polite to refuse! It can be worth allowing a class a period of time in which to choose who will represent them, and providing some contact time to discuss what is involved, and maybe to facilitate a ballot or election.

2   **Remember that the student(s) chosen may be somewhat in awe of the committee.** Students can feel uncomfortable in a gathering of so many highly qualified academics, and this can lead them to be observers rather than true participants in the processes of meetings.

3   **Take care when putting student representatives on the spot.** They won't necessarily be able to speak at once on behalf of their classmates. They may be able to give their own personal views (which of course are valuable in their own right), but you may need to allow them time to find out the opinion of their colleagues before reporting back to a future meeting of the committee or board.

4   **Allow student representatives to contribute to the agenda-forming process.** When they are given time to supply suggestions for the agenda of a future meeting, they have the chance to discuss the matter with fellow students, and the ownership of the representation is duly enhanced.

5 **Be prepared to give student representatives responsibilities for researching particular views of their classmates.** It is important that this does not become burdensome to them. It helps, however, when they have definite purposes underpinning each stage of their liaison with their fellow students. Student reps can, for example, have more success at getting a good response rate from a questionnaire to the class, especially if entrusted and briefed to make their own preliminary analysis of the findings *before* giving in the completed questionnaires.

6 **Treat student representatives as full committee members.** This means, for example, ensuring that they receive 'Notice of Meetings', agendas, and minutes in the same ways as academic members of the committee. They should also feel at liberty to show any of the documentation to fellow students.

7 **Make sure student reps' comments and contributions are minuted accurately.** Even if they make controversial comments, the fact that they are being minuted acts as an appropriate restraining process. Also, this helps the student reps themselves prove to the students they are representing that they have indeed followed through matters at the committee.

8 **Don't cut student reps off in mid-flow!** It may have taken them considerable courage (maybe backed by substantial preparation or research) before they make an impassioned plea or complaint or suggestion. Courtesy demands that they are given at least as much chance to have their say as anyone else.

9 **Don't let student reps become overburdened with duties and commitments.** Remember that they are also studying, and it is tragic if their studies suffer significantly as a result of the energies and time they put into representing fellow students.

10 **Consider ways in which student reps may gain academic credit for their role.** For example, this could be done as a project module in an independent studies pathway. Many student union branches are looking at accreditation of the student representative role. Alternatively, consider finding ways of including the service of student reps into student profiles or records of achievement.

11 **Remember to thank student representatives for their time and their work.** It is important that they feel that their role is valued, and not just a ritual for appearance's sake. As well as verbal appreciation at meetings, it is worth sending each student representative an official 'thank you' letter when terms of office are completed.

Chapter 6   Preparing For Quality Assessment Visits

We should point out at the outset of this chapter that most of our suggestions here are relevant to the teaching quality assessment processes and practices currently in operation in the UK. Nevertheless, we are aware of very similar moves about quality assurance taking place in several other parts of the world, and we trust that the suggestions in this chapter will be found relevant in most places where there is a systematic quest towards enhancing the quality of teaching, learning and assessment in higher education.

In the systems used in the UK, the 'quality visit' has become quite an auspicious occasion, and we begin this chapter by offering an extended set of suggestions to staff in schools or departments regarding how best they may prepare to be seen to be succeeding when visited. We would like to point out, however, that all of the suggestions we have made under this heading are things that should ideally be happening anyway as part of a drive towards quality enhancement, and should not just be preparations for a particularly visible element of performance. We next include an extended set of suggestions which are specific to the current processes of teaching quality assessment in England: 'Writing a self-assessment document', where our aim is to help colleagues set the scene for their quality visits in a realistic and efficient way. We continue with some pointers about how to ensure that 'Quality on the day' is evidenced in the event of a quality assessment visit.

We continue this chapter by offering some suggestions regarding the quality enhancement of library and computing services. Such services are inextricably tied up to the quality of teaching and learning. We have based our suggestions on specific briefings which are suggested to teaching quality assessors/ reviewers visiting institutions in England, but which are sufficiently translatable to provide a quality agenda for libraries and computing services in most contexts elsewhere.

One of the things that seems to be a highly significant part of teaching quality assessment visits is the process of teaching actually being observed by people from outside the institution. This leads us into a series of no less than six sets of suggestions about observation of teaching, many of which are based on the briefing materials provided to teaching quality assessors in the UK. We would argue, however, that even without any prospect of external observation of teaching, it is worthwhile to implement all of these suggestions to promote a climate where internal observation of teaching is a natural part of the culture of an institution, and a major source of information about good (and bad) practice to fuel the processes of quality enhancement. In several parts of these sets of suggestions, we overlap with, then extend to, the observation dimension some of the general suggestions we made in Chapter 3 about enhancing the quality of teaching processes.

36

Preparing for quality visits

Quality assessment visits, organised by the relevant Funding Councils, are certainly here to stay over the next few years. Appropriate preparation can help to ensure a greater likelihood of a positive outcome, and can help to reduce the stress levels of everyone involved.

1 **Recognise that it is worth spending some time preparing.** It is all too easy to be so busy with everyday matters that it's tempting to take the attitude 'they'll just have to take us as they find us'.

2 **Prepare well in advance.** It is never too early to start. Devise a strategy and action plans, working out target dates for each major task, and spreading responsibilities in ways that help to ensure that staff take on ownership of the processes.

3 **Prepare for a visit that you're not yet having!** When the sorts of actions that are involved in preparing for quality visits are not special, but are part of the normal day-to-day life of an institution, the distance between 'where you are' and 'where you want to be seen to have reached' is narrowed continuously, and the anxiety which can be caused by an impending spotlight is reduced.

4 **Let everyone know – raise consciousness.** Don't assume this only involves academic staff. It requires a team effort from the start, including everyone from porters to senior management. Different kinds of briefing may be appropriate. Don't forget to keep people informed and updated throughout the process.

5 **Think about the statistics – get the figures right.** If standard procedures do not exist to collate statistical information, try to set them in place. Accurate data is essential, but can be very time-consuming to collect. It may be sensible to allocate this job to one or more people.

6   **Involve the learning support services.** We need to work collaboratively, and their support is vital. Have the learning support services met as a group before? What do they see as the issues? Are they clear about the roles expected of them during a visit?

7   **Promote peer observation and review.** Teaching staff may feel very apprehensive about being visited and may need a lot of reassurance. Set up support groups and encourage discussion of the advantages of peer observation. Setting up peer observation training sessions can be really beneficial. Use existing videos of different teaching scenarios, and ask participants what feedback they would give to the lecturers they see. Advise them always to start with positive feedback, for example giving three positive comments for every 'could do better'. Help them to gain practice in observation and feedback skills; this will improve confidence levels for when the inspection occurs.

8   **Make full use of people who have done it all before.** There are likely to be colleagues close to home who have been involved in past visits, or who are involved as visitors themselves elsewhere. Their experience is far too valuable to waste. Avoid reinventing the wheel, when there is experience around to draw on.

9   **Avoid complacency based on past success.** Even if past visits have resulted in very positive outcomes, the next visit will almost certainly involve different people, and they may not be looking for the same things as happened previously. Other places will have moved on since your last visit, and expectations of visitors will have increased.

10 **Avoid despair based on previous failures.** Even when a previous visit has been traumatic, this does not necessarily mean that the next one will be a disaster. Many things may have improved since that time, and because this can happen gradually, the home team may not be aware of the scale of the advances made. Also, the visitors are likely to have gained further experience in what reasonably to expect, and may be less inclined to be critical.

11 **Get a team spirit going.** When colleagues are pulling together constructively, the impression they create is always much more favourable than when there are conflicting attitudes and approaches in an institution. It is important that everyone feels part of the team, and that there isn't a top-down ethos where colleagues may lose any sense of ownership of their responsibility for ensuring that the outcomes are favourable.

12 **Spring-clean.** Apply a fresh eye to the environment. Could old equipment and furniture be replaced? Would the budget run to a new coat of paint? Can the clutter be disposed of? Would posters and pictures soften the atmosphere?

13 **Check the paperwork.** It is essential that all the required paperwork is available and up to date. Read the full documentation from the inspecting authority, to ensure that you have left no stone unturned. Read past overview reports, available in the UK on the World Wide Web.

14 **Don't get it out of proportion.** It is unwise to have endless, long meetings about preparing for a visit. Frequent, very short meetings work better. Make sure each meeting has a small but definite purpose, rather than having meetings with so much on the agenda that nothing actually gets achieved.

15 **Provide briefings.** Staff usually want to be involved, so face-to-face and written briefings are likely to be appreciated. Pace the information, and don't overload your colleagues. Be aware of the different audiences, deans, heads of department, technicians, support staff, porters, the learning support team and so on.

16 **Learn through collaboration and networking.** Make full use of your informal contacts in other institutions to gather experience of assessment visits. Despite the competition that may exist between institutions, there is a wealth of informal contact between professional people at all levels in institutions.

17 **Make progress happen.** There won't always be unanimous agreement about every issue to be discussed in your preparations for a visit. It is important to avoid bickering on trying to resolve the unresolvable, and make compromise decisions which everyone is prepared to live with for the purpose of the visit.

18 **Distinguish between the urgent and the important.** Not everything that seems urgent is important, and not everything that is important is urgent. When creating the agenda for decisions to be made in preparation for the visit, make sure that the important issues get a fair hearing.

19 **Don't try to solve every problem overnight.** It is often enough that a problem has been diagnosed, and an action plan has been devised to address it, rather than that a solution to the problem has been hastily put in place prior to a visit.

20 **Think about rehearsals.** It is said that 75% of the success of an event is achieved before the arrival of the visiting assessors. A run-through gives people confidence, identifies the issues which need addressing, and helps to reduce stress on the day. Use people who can give each other effective and supportive feedback, at the same time as identifying problematic areas.

21 **Plan the first few hours very carefully.** There will be no second chance to make a good first impression. Try to arrange that the sun will be shining (metaphorically speaking) in every way that you can during this vital period.

37

Writing a self-assessment document

The UK system of quality assessment requires departments which are to have the quality of their teaching and learning reviewed to produce a self-assessment document. This provides the basis for a quality assessment visit by a team of assessors/reviewers. The following tips are designed to help departments about to be reviewed to write such a document effectively. They are based on the *Assessors Handbook* (HEFCE, 1996) which should be referred to in detail by those undergoing the process.

1   **Think carefully about the picture you want to paint of your department.** The self-assessment document provides an opportunity for departments to make a case for what they do. In a prescribed format, it enables those who know best the courses and modules being assessed to provide a basis for evaluation. Assessment is made against the institution's own aims and objectives. This avoids the irrelevance of assessment against externally imposed criteria and enables account to be taken of diversity across institutions.

2   **Remember that the self-assessment document will set the agenda for the visit.** Whatever you claim will provide the framework of what quality assessors will review. They are likely to look for gaps, inconsistencies, problems and places where key issues are raised.

3   **Self-assessment should be analytical.** The aim is not just to provide a narrative account of a department's achievements, but to portray an actively self-critical and self-improving process rather than one which is complacent, static or unaware. A self-assessment that implies there are no problems will not look credible.

4   **Start data collection early.** Writing the necessary documentation can be a gruelling task and one of the biggest jobs can be actually locating all the figures and information needed. Use existing documentation wherever possible as a basis for the paper.

5   **Aim to write very concisely.** Be prepared to be very selective about what you include and use tables and graphs in the annexes where possible. Use bullet points as appropriate (but be aware that a bullet counts as a word under HEFCE rules!)

6   **Stick to the guidelines.** Very specific guidance on the format and size of the self-assessment documentation is provided in the current HEFCE circulars. Do not exceed (or undershoot) the word length as the documentation is likely to be sent back if the guidelines are not strictly adhered to (and it isn't enough to change the font size and resubmit, as one university found to its peril!)

7   **Consider getting help before starting to assemble paperwork.** Your own institution's educational development service (if it has one) may have considerable experience in helping people prepare for quality assessment. Alternatively, it can be well worth bringing in similar personnel from outside the institution.

8   **Don't give the task of preparing the self-assessment document to one person alone.** An individual is likely to be too close to the task and may not be able to have a clear overview. With a team of one, important points can be over looked or scantily treated. A working group with shared responsibilities and duties is best suited to the task.

9   **Get feedback on the document throughout its development.** The more people you can involve in polishing and tuning the self-assessment document, the less likely it is that you will be surprised or dismayed by the reactions of the document's intended recipients in due course.

10   **Let one person have final responsibility for the ultimate version of the document.** Otherwise it may end up as a hotchpotch of elements without cohesion. One person needs to ensure a single authorial voice throughout the paper.

11   **Use someone outside the preparation process to review your document once it is written.** Brief this person to look for areas which are not fully explained or documented. Remedy them if possible within the limits of space in the document or note them carefully to help you prepare for questioning on the day of the visit.

12 **Make sure that the document is impeccably produced.** Typographical errors, poor layout and discontinuities will all give a poor impression of the department even before the quality assessors visit.

13 **Be aware that assessors will have available to them documentation other than the self-assessment.** All data published by the university is likely to be scrutinised by the assessors. It is therefore important that they are not faced with contradictory claims.

14 **Start with the mission statement of your institution.** Whatever your institution claims to be and do should be reflected in your self-assessment document. This can provide difficulties when the university has a published mission statement that is unwieldy or imprecise, but it should provide your starting point. Quality assessors are not in the business of judging mission statements: their task is to judge how well these have been interpreted locally into teaching and learning provision.

15 **Make clear links between the different elements of the documentation.** It should be possible to see how the university mission statement, subject rationale, subject aims, subject objectives, course aims and course objectives all link together. These in turn should link to session aims and objectives when individual classes are observed.

16 **Define your subject rationale.** This is likely to be fairly brief and should clearly articulate the reasons why the subject is being taught here and in this particular context. If the rationale doesn't address all aspects of the mission, (as, indeed, it often would not be expected to) you should clarify why this is the case.

17 **Define your subject aims.** These should be a statement of the broad direction to be taken into the teaching and learning process which is directly linked into the module/course/programme rationale. Aims are usually expressed in terms of the sorts of abilities, knowledge and attitudes that stakeholders in higher education can normally expect of a student who successfully completes a course of study in this area.

18 **Outline your subject objectives/outcomes.** These tend to be more specific and tend to be closely linked to separate components of the teaching and learning experience. Objectives relate to the acquisition of knowledge, development of understanding, conceptual, intellectual and subject-specific skills, the development of generic transferable skills, the development of values, of motivation and positive attitudes to learning.

19   **Link these to your course aims and objectives.** It should be evident in your documentation that the mission, rationale, aims and objectives of the university and department are clearly translated into what you actually teach and assess. Inevitably there will be overlap between course and subject aims and objectives, so care will be needed in the writing of them to avoid repetition.

20   **Keep in mind that teaching and learning are (or should be) inseparable.** Teaching involves the whole management and promotion of student learning, using a wide variety of methods including independent learning and the use of all kinds of learning resources.

21   **Ensure that your teaching and learning aims are SMART.** They should be Specific, Measurable, Achievable, Realistic and Timed. Expressed aims that are woolly, vague, indefinable and unrealistic will weaken your case, as will claims that oversell your provision or which are too modest.

22   **Draw clear links between learning outcomes and assessment processes and instruments.** Quality assessors/reviewers will need to be able to see clearly how you assess whether students have achieved what you claim they will. Discrepancies between the teaching and learning processes and the ways in which they are assessed will be unhelpful to your case.

23   **Identify and assess what is distinctive about your subject.** You need clear vision about what you are aiming to achieve and why. If you claim in your documentation, for example, that you have a distinctive international focus for your teaching, this should be clearly evidenced in the curriculum as well as the prospectus.

24   **Provide profiles of staff and students and information about learning resources available.** These can be supported by tables, graphs and other data in the annexes at the end of the document.

25   **Evaluate the quality of your educational provision.** The six aspects of provision that the UK system requires to be covered are curriculum design, content and organisation, teaching, learning and assessment, student progression and achievement, student support and guidance, learning resources and quality assurance and enhancement.

26   **Provide documentary evidence of your achievements.** It isn't enough merely to claim that your teaching in the department is underpinned by world-class research. Evidence for this should be provided in the form of specific examples or with outcomes from the research assessment exercise, for example. You can also provide employment statistics, student and employer feedback, evidence of access, international and disabled students performing well, and so on.

27   **Provide in annexes additional material required.** Guidance on these is also given and they are likely to include statistical indicators, the structure of the provision, details of modular schemes where applicable, information about partnerships of various kinds, and so on. Don't send extraneous material that is not asked for.

28   **Don't ignore the problems.** By the time quality assessors / reviewers have read all your documentation and talked to staff and students they are likely to have a clear idea of anything that might be going wrong in your department, so it is futile to pretend problems don't exist.

29   **State clearly what you plan to do about any areas of difficulty.** Quality assessors are likely to be more impressed by proposals of action to be taken on problem issues and areas of difficulty than by head-in-the-sand attitudes that ignore difficult areas.

30   **Learn from those who have undergone the process already.** HEFCE make available in paper and electronic formats all the extant assessment reports from departments who have already been assessed. You can learn a lot from reading these. Purchase them from HEFCE or view them on the HEFCE Web pages.

38

Quality on the day

The following suggestions may help make a quality visit go that little bit more smoothly, and can certainly make the visitors feel more welcome.

1   **Appoint a 'welcome' person.** A friendly, named person who is the contact point at the beginning, middle, and end of the day is very reassuring. This also means one person can keep a grip on what is happening. Such a person will need a stout pair of shoes, a good telephone manner, flexibility and friendliness at all times.

2   **Prepare the base rooms.** A welcoming, well-equipped base room for the assessors will certainly help. It needs to be private, well stocked with drinks (hot and cold) and snacks. Such a room needs a telephone, photocopier, surfaces to write on, boxes with the information for perusal, and space to lay out samples of students' work.

3   **Look after creature comforts.** Make sure your quality assessors have everything they need in the way of communications equipment, paper and consumables of all kinds. Make sure their base room is warm enough in winter or well ventilated (or air-conditioned) in summer. Make sure their travel arrangements home are catered for (have timetables and taxi numbers to hand).

4   **Plan for emergencies.** Such things as train strikes, go-slows, broken lifts, ill relatives and headaches can all disrupt a visit. All these are traumatic – as is a photocopier which breaks down! Check whether any other special events are happening on the day. Make arrangements to cover equipment failures and so on.

5   **Keep the channels of communication going.** Events can change suddenly – be prepared for this. You may need to reschedule staff because of changing circumstances. The assessors may realise that they have sufficient information on a topic and wish to change the focus. Additional paper information may be sought, or a request be made to interview a particular member of staff.

6   **Offer a support mechanism.** Occasionally things may not go according to plan. Someone may feel unwell but struggle on. A lecture may go badly or students may be unusually quiet. A sympathetic ear and a strong cup of tea may do the trick, so order extra tea bags!

7   **Keep an ear to the ground.** The tone of a visit can change suddenly. Watch the body language, and listen carefully to requests. Be flexible, and pass on messages where appropriate.

8   **Brief everyone.** It's important that all categories of staff know what is going on, and are prepared to contribute to the process.

9   **Make sure that internal visits run smoothly.** Plan so that trips to the library, IT centre, educational development service and other venues run smoothly as part of the quality appraisal event. Involve staff from these areas in the preparation for the event, and in the planning of the venues seen by the visitors.

10 **Keep an eye on loose cannons**. If you feel you have people who are likely to be destructive on the day, don't try to hide them or over-compensate for their actions or views, or send them off on a field trip! Quality assessors are not fools and will be able to tell the difference between those with a genuine grievance or problem, and troublemakers.

39

Quality of library and computing services

Because of the close connections between many aspects of library, learning resource centres, and computer services provision, we have combined our discussion of all of these in the next section. The following suggestions are based on recommendations drawn together by the University Librarians Group (SCONUL, Standing Conference of University Librarians) and the University Computer Services Heads Group (UCISA) together with the Teaching Quality Assessment division of HEFCE.

1   **Check the connections between library and computer services to course development and review.** It helps a great deal if there are representatives from the library and computer services on course boards, and particularly at review and validation events.

2   **Library and computer services staff need to be seen to communicate together effectively.** In institutions where the services have already been combined, this should not pose any problems. However, problems have been known when the services have remained separate, for example when different specifications and standards of computing equipment are used in the respective departments.

3   **Ensure that support service staff communicate effectively with academic staff.** Teaching quality assessors/reviewers are likely to talk to both teaching staff and support staff, and will notice quickly if there are any discrepancies in the information they receive from each source. It is best to be able to demonstrate clear mechanisms whereby support service staff are kept aware of the requirements on them, such as in changing courses.

4   **Give library and support services staff opportunities to contribute to student induction and staff induction programmes.** This can do much to establish an appropriate level of understanding and communication between library staff, support services staff, and academic staff and students. It is also worth ensuring that teaching staff are given opportunities to contribute to support-staff training programmes, for example to help to keep them informed about future patterns of teaching, new uses of resource-based learning, and so on.

5   **Have clear open lines of communication between students and library staff and computer services staff.** Student feedback plays an important role in quality enhancement of academic programmes, and is equally important to ensure that libraries, learning resource centres and computing services function well.

6   **Ensure that students are actively encouraged to make full use of the facilities available to them in libraries and computing centres.** It is often the case that students are so busy trying to keep up to date with their coursework and assessments that they do not know the range of help and facilities available to them in libraries and computing centres. It is useful to proactively inform and encourage students about the resources at their disposal.

7   **Give students a good reason to learn about resources available**. Consider making completion of an independent learning workbook on information services an assessed element of every first year course, so that students are obliged to find their way around information retrieval facilities for themselves very early in their studies.

8   **Give new staff more than a chat at induction.** While it can be useful for them to have a short talk by a senior member of the library and the computing service, this only really serves to give them one or two faces they may remember. It is better to include a short tour of the facilities as part of staff induction programmes.

9   **Library and computing support needs to match course requirements.** Teaching quality assessors/reviewers are likely to probe whether the resources are sufficient in quantity and appropriate in quality for students on the courses of the institution.

10   **Have clear and appropriate mechanisms for the selection of learning resource materials and equipment.** The systems by which teaching staff are involved in the most appropriate selection of materials may need to be checked and improved, especially where resources are tight and hard decisions have to be made.

11   **Check that the availability of facilities and resources is sufficient to match student needs.** Desk collections, or reference-only stock are ways of coping with high student demand for particular resources. With computing equipment, tracking the usage and availability of terminals and machines is an important step towards trying to meet demand and extend the opportunities for students to use equipment.

12   **Ensure that the pressures on library study space are monitored.** It is important to be able to show that every attempt has been made to make sufficient space available to students, particularly towards examinations time, and extending opening hours is one way of meeting their needs at such times.

13   **User support needs to be available to both students and staff.** Do a survey of the skills training available relating to effective use of the library and the computing facilities available. Help-desks and help-lines are a visible sign of such support, and feedback should be gathered about how effective the training and support is in practice.

14   **Help staff ask for the support they need**. Sometimes staff are embarrassed to ask for help from more junior staff or if students are around, because they don't want to look foolish. Develop sensitive mechanisms where seeking support doesn't call attention to the user.

15   **Ensure that appropriate support is available to all groups of students.** Library and computing facilities and support need to be suitable not only to full-time students, but also to students who are studying part-time, or by distance learning. Disabled students should be catered for in whatever ways are most suitable for them.

16   **Staff training programmes are an indicator of the intention to achieve quality enhancement.** All computing and library staff should have opportunities to participate in relevant and appropriate staff development activities, and the effectiveness of these should be monitored.

17   **Consider co-training of staff**. Information services staff of all kinds can often benefit from training together and training each other, whether this is using new equipment, learning new packages and applications or on how to run one-to-one or small-group training.

18   **Monitor the effectiveness of library and computing services as seen by academic staff.** It is useful to conduct regular surveys of the staff who make most use of the facilities, as well as trying to find out the reactions of those staff who make little use of them.

19 **Gather student feedback about their experiences of using the library and computing services.** This can usefully be combined with school or departmental mechanisms for gathering and analysing student feedback as well as helping in the process of continuous quality improvement of services.

20 **Advise staff on how to spend their money**. Often the people who buy computer equipment are not completely up to date with technology, and costly mistakes can be made by making unwise or inappropriate purchasing decisions. Some institutions only permit purchases of IT equipment through central agencies, which can be frustrating for individuals, but can enable good cost savings through negotiated contracts with suppliers, and can ensure informed decisions.

21 **Help staff to learn to use the equipment they purchase.** Consider providing an 'unpack, install and advise' service for staff, to prevent the wastefulness of untrained (often quite senior) staff attempting to set up and use unfamiliar equipment and then taking ages to learn how to use it properly.

22 **Don't forget that quality enhancement applies to many other services.** In a book of this kind, it would be impossible for us to go into factors relating quality enhancement to, for example, media services, learning resource production services, television studio provision, student services, accommodation services and so on, as such provision is usually organised in very different ways in different institutions. The most useful way to link institutional or departmental quality enhancement issues to the wide range of services is by careful linking of matters relating to teaching, learning and assessment to the roles of each of these services in particular course or institutional contexts.

40

Practising for observation

Quality visits can be stressful for staff (and students) who are normally busy enough without the additional dimension of strangers watching them or talking to them. It can be very reassuring in setting up practice for observation if there is a guarantee of confidentiality, so that detailed feedback is only given to the person being observed, with feedback to whole groups being constrained to that of a generic nature. The following suggestions may help reduce the additional stresses that quality visits can cause.

1   **Remember that most learning happens by doing.** Talking about being visited has limited payoff compared to actually having being visited. Practice runs with staff from the home team role-playing visitors can help everyone get used to the feel of being visited.

2   **Practise the right game.** Use all the local experience that may be available within your home institution to make sure that mock visits are as close as possible to the agendas that you will address in a real visit. It is useful to get used to taking critical feedback from someone you know, as preparation to taking it well from someone you don't know. It is useful to actively encourage staff from other parts of the institution, who already have some experience regarding quality visits, to make this experience useful to you.

3   **Don't allow practising to go wrong.** Sometimes it is harder to take critical feedback from someone you know than from someone vested with authority from outside. The criticism may be just as valid, however! Make sure that everyone involved in mock visits feels that the visitors are allowed to role-play rather than make enemies.

4   **Build in appropriate practice into the normal operation of the institution.** This means that when the practice is really needed, prior to a real visit, for example, it is much easier to find the time for it to happen. It also means that many of the potential problems will have already been recognised and dealt with.

5   **Involve everyone.** It is important that the ownership of the responsibility for preparing for quality visits does not rest with one or two individuals. While it may give some satisfaction to have a focus for blame if things should go wrong, it is better to have everyone sharing in the determination to plan that things will go well.

6   **Involve students.** Give students practice in giving feedback to visitors by getting them to give you the same sorts of feedback as they may be asked for by visitors. Explain why you welcome their comments, and then tell them what you will intend to do differently as a result of their feedback.

7   **Always give positive feedback first.** When role-playing a visitor, help put staff at ease by giving the good news first (and indeed making sure there is always some good news!). We are all much more likely to take on board the 'could do betters' if we have received the positive statements first.

8   **Give three positives for every one 'could do better'.** Even when there is much to comment adversely on, it is important to give sufficient good news. If people are given too much adverse comment, they may lose track of which are the most important parts of the agenda that they need to address.

9   **Think about fears and aspirations regarding an observation.** A general discussion in a group can help to allay fears and raise issues that can be talked about in an open and constructive way.

10 **Treat observation as free consultancy.** 'Isn't it wonderful to have a colleague or friend who finds time to engage in an educational conversation with us?' is a much better approach than 'I haven't time for all this practising, let's just hope it goes alright on the day!'

41

Making use of feedback from observers

Feedback on the observation of teaching can be a major contributor to the processes which lead to quality enhancement. The following suggestions are intended to help the feedback be received in the appropriate spirit.

1   **Promote the attitude that all feedback is potentially useful.** Feedback is an important part of everyday learning, and it is constructive to regard quality visits not so much in terms of the verdicts which may be reached, but in terms of the availability of valuable feedback which they may bring.

2   **Make a video of part of a feedback session.** Use this to show that such sessions can be very positive give and take discussions.

3   **Be prepared to receive positive feedback.** In many cultures, there is a sense of embarrassment when receiving praise. This leads people to shrug it off, and to fail to really take on board the value of finding out more about what is regarded as successful. It is worth practising *receiving* positive feedback, verbally acknowledging it, and thanking the people who deliver it.

4   **Get practising for receiving negative feedback.** Regard criticism as useful feedback. Avoid the temptations to become hostile, or to justify one's position, or to make excuses for things that were found to be lacking. When critical feedback is felt to have been openly received and taken note of, the people giving such feedback are much more satisfied that their job has been done effectively, than when they are not at all sure that the feedback has been listened to and heeded.

5   **Practise eliciting feedback.** Gain skills in drawing out feedback, and get the people giving it to clarify it and expand on it when necessary. 'What do you consider the best thing about the way we are handling so-and-so?' and 'What is the first thing about this that you would suggest we try to change?' are the sort of questions that help in this process.

6   **Provide opportunities for feedback to be delivered.** In planning a visit, it can be useful to timetable frequent and appropriate feedback opportunities, particularly for the sort of interim feedback that is often possible at stages before the visiting team may retire to consider their final verdicts. It can be useful to plan that such interim feedback elements can be quite short in duration, to avoid the embarrassment to the visiting team should they not yet be ready to deliver much feedback at the stage concerned.

7   **Make case studies out of existing feedback.** Use any published feedback from other institutions as a means of developing the skills of interpreting feedback comments, role-playing responses to such feedback and the decision-making that would have been appropriate on the basis of such feedback. All this paves the way to being better-able to deal with the real feedback you will derive from quality visits.

8   **Share the feedback with your learners.** Students like to feel involved. Explain why you might be doing something different – this could lead to more feedback.

9   **Share the feedback with your colleagues.** It may be that colleague's views are usefully shared. This can lead to economical use of resources or make a stronger case for a staff development event, or a claim for additional resources.

10   **Use feedback as part of the appraisal process.** Making good use of feedback during an appraisal conversation can enhance the educational discussion and help you to clarify your own thinking.

11   **Use feedback to set yourself a target.** Use feedback as an opportunity to enhance some aspect of your work. It may be simply to set aside time to read, or to try out a new teaching technique.

42

Preparing new staff for observation

Staff new to teaching are often apprehensive about anyone watching their teaching performance, and may be even more scared at the prospect of outsiders making formal appraisals of their work. The following suggestions aim to address these problems.

1 **Include teaching observation in induction training programmes.** The sooner that staff become accustomed to the experience of other people watching their teaching performance, the greater their confidence becomes at handling such situations.

2 **Start off with non-threatening situations.** For example, getting new teaching staff to do short teaching elements with groups of their peers is less intimidating than having real teaching sessions observed.

3 **Start off with a basic agenda for observation.** Avoid the situation of the performances of new staff being observed against a framework of detailed criteria intended for practised and experienced teachers. Develop the criteria gradually, preferably by allowing groups of new staff to formulate their own benchmarks, giving them a sense of ownership of the process of observation of their teaching.

4 **Make sure that not too much emphasis is placed on presentation skills.** Include room for the quality of handouts, overheads, media elements and class exercises to be covered in the observation criteria. This can help spread the load, so that new staff are not overly anxious about their presentation skills until they begin to develop more confidence in giving presentations.

5   **Remind staff that in real life they are not being observed every second.** While it is possible that some students will notice slips they may make, they are unlikely to have the undivided attention of the whole class at any such time (or any other time!).

6   **Encourage new staff to take every opportunity to observe others' teaching.** Alert them to how easy it is to pick up ideas of good practice to try out in their own work, and also things to avoid in their own work.

7   **Get new staff to do some structured observation during departmental or college events.** Guest lecturers may not expect to be observed at such times, but such observation can be done quite inconspicuously, with a debriefing session after the event to exchange notes between observers.

8   **Use videos of 'neutral others'.** A number of videos of staff teaching already exist. Use one of these and ask for comments. It seems easier to observe strangers rather than peers.

9   **Provide opportunities for a variety of situations to be observed.** These could include the large lecture, seminars, laboratory classes and so on.

10   **Give staff an opportunity to give themselves feedback.** We are all experienced observers – we did start from early childhood. Giving ourselves feedback is a good prerequisite to giving others feedback.

43

Motivating experienced staff regarding teaching observation

Experienced staff should not feel threatened by the prospect of their teaching been observed, but they often feel that it is an insult to their professional integrity to be scrutinised in the way they work. The following suggestions can help overcome such barriers.

1   **Identify benefits which will appeal to experienced staff.** For example, they may be heading towards formal observation of elements of their teaching as part of teaching quality assessments. Remind them how much better it is for any matters that may cause problems to be discovered before it counts officially.

2   **Remind staff of the possibility of getting into a rut.** When anyone has been teaching a particular topic for a considerable time, it is natural to tend to go on autopilot, and be less aware of what is actually happening during teaching sessions.

3   **Get experienced staff into observing others' teaching.** For example, involve them in observing new staff as part of staff development programmes. The act of applying some quality criteria to others' teaching is an effective way of reminding one about how one's own teaching lives up to such criteria.

4   **Encourage team teaching.** When experienced staff are regularly in the position of observing parts of their colleagues' teaching, a considerable amount of automatic staff development occurs as they learn from each others' triumphs and disasters!

5   **Build teaching observation into appraisal procedures.** If, for example, a discussion of the results of peer observation is part of each annual appraisal interview, everyone is more likely to participate in observation, and the way that it is planned and timetabled can be left to staff to arrange in their own ways.

6   **Tell them it's free consultancy!** Where else could someone give you their full attention for at least one hour and not send you the bill!

7   **Explain how quick the process is.** Suppose an observer gives you three tips at the end of an hour; this can be very good value compared to just reading a book on teaching practices, where you may not happen to read the things you may most need to find out.

8   **Explain how students could become more motivated by the spin-off from observation.** Being observed can help staff to reflect on how they could do something better or in a different way that can help students become more involved in their own learning process.

9   **Suggest that their students can become better learners.** Being observed, and receiving and analysing feedback makes us more aware of how we learn, and this can be passed on to students, whose success may depend on their expertise as learners as well as subject-specific scholars.

10 **Talk to them about the advantages of lifelong learning.** To learn a new skill, read a new book, or try a new method of assessment can all be rewarding parts of the job of teachers in further and higher education.

44

Working out which qualities to observe in lectures

It would be boring for students if all of their lectures were conducted to a standard specification. However, there are many factors which can contribute to successful and productive lectures, and the following questions may offer a starting point for observation checklists for large-group sessions.

1   **How well were the intended learning outcomes of the session communicated?** Did the lecturer make it clear to students what they should gain from the lecture, and where the topic fits into the overall course?

2   **Was the lecturer clearly audible?** Was the voice quality such that students for whom English is a second language could keep up with the wording? Was it possible for students in the most distant parts of the room to hear clearly?

3   **Was the lecture relevant?** It is worth checking that lectures make good use of the face-to-face contact with students, and avoid going off on tangents away from the central agenda of the syllabus.

4   **Did the lecture hold students' attention well?** It is easy for an observer to notice from students' expressions and body language when their attention is straying. It is not as easy for lecturers themselves to be aware of this, as the students nearest them are more likely to be attentive (or at least looking attentive!)

5   **Was the lecture sufficiently interactive?** The sorts of interaction which may be desirable include making sure that students have the opportunity to ask questions or seek clarification, and activities in the lecture period where students learn by doing tasks or solving problems, then gain feedback from the lecturer and from each other on how successfully they did such tasks.

6   **Was the lecture well structured?** In a coherent lecture, it is possible to follow how the agenda set at the beginning unfolds and develops, and to remain aware of the purposes of the whole lecture as each part occurs. Was the structure outlined in ways that helped students to make useful notes? Were there cues to distinguish key points from elaboration? Were visual devices used to emphasise key words, phrases and definitions? Were explanations and relationships developed through the use of diagrams?

7   **Did the lecture remind students of what they should already have understood from previous work?** One of the useful dividends of a well structured large-group session is that students can gain reminders about the things they are expected to have mastered already from previous lectures.

8   **Did the lecturer have a suitable range of techniques for dealing with students' questions?** For example, it is useful to be able to respond to some questions straightaway. When this is not possible, ways round the problem include agreeing to report back on a future occasion, perhaps asking the rest of the group to research the answer to a question as well.

9   **Did the session come to a robust conclusion?** A danger is that some lectures just seem to peter out, without coming to a definite and hopefully memorable conclusion. One way of signifying the end of a lecture is to go back and check whether students feel they have now achieved the intended learning outcomes.

10   **Did the lecturer seek feedback from students?** It's too late to leave such feedback to the end of a whole series of lectures, or the end of a course. When lecturers gain student feedback intermittently during a series, they are able to fine-tune the progression in line with students' reactions and comments. It is, however, important to avoid boring the students by using the same feedback device (however well it may work) repeatedly.

45

Working out what to observe in small-group teaching

It is likely that in a quality visit there will be some occasion to observe directly what happens in small-group sessions. Sometimes, attempts to observe such sessions may interfere with the processes involved. However, quality assessors/reviewers may wish to ascertain how well small-group teaching and learning is proceeding, when preparing for a visit, and it is worth bearing in mind the ways that they will approach this.

1   **Make the intended learning outcomes of small-group sessions clear to students.** It is important to make such outcomes significantly different from those associated with large-group or whole-class sessions. Normally, small-group learning can be expected to deepen, broaden, or extend the learning that students achieve in large-group sessions. Documentation of the outcomes associated with small-group teaching and learning is a useful indicator to visitors of the quality of such provision. It is useful to provide students with written guidance notes on the content and purposes of the small-group elements of their programmes of study. Such notes can include details of pre-reading and assignments.

2   **Clarify what you mean by tutorial and seminar.** Concepts of these kinds of teaching–learning situations tend to overlap, and also to vary with the nature of subjects and disciplines. Visitors may well enquire about how seminars differ from tutorials, and how students are advised to prepare appropriately for each situation.

3   **Collect evidence of the tasks students do in small-group sessions.** Assessors can gain a good deal from seeing the briefings and documentation relating to small-group tutorials or seminar programmes. Conversely, in the absence of any such evidence, they may infer that the quality of such sessions is not a priority in your course.

4   **Gather student feedback about the value to them of small-group sessions.** This not only helps you to continually enhance the benefit of such sessions, but is useful evidence to show to visitors that you are conducting such sessions effectively.

5   **Consider collecting evidence relating to the way such sessions actually work.** For example, it can be useful to make sample video-recordings of suitably chosen, important sessions. These can be used to prepare future students for the sort of experience they should expect from small-group work, but can also be used as evidence of the nature and quality of such occasions. Students' behaviour is much less influenced by the presence of an unobtrusively situated camcorder, than by a quality assessor!

6   **Be ready to show that the learning that is associated with small-group sessions is taken seriously.** For example, make transparent the links between the intended learning outcomes of such sessions and the assessment agenda. If students (and assessors) can see how the learning intended in small-group sessions is assessed, they will take such provision more seriously and give them better preparation and participation.

7   **Focus in on specific aspects.** The opening and closure of a small group session can both be vital to its success. Spotlighting such aspects can concentrate the mind, and bring key issues to the surface.

8   **Note the differences between small-group work and large-group lectures.** List the differences and similarities. Check that full use is being made of the opportunities for interaction which come with small groups.

9   **Focus on the learners.** Do you give opportunities for students to lead the sessions, putting the emphasis on them to take responsibility for their learning? This can also encourage them to take their preparation for small-group work more seriously. It can be valuable to give students opportunities to talk without the tutor overhearing, allowing them to develop ideas without the fear of looking silly.

10 **Appreciate differences in approaches to learning.** Some students enjoy active participation, while others prefer to reflect and some want to know the theoretical underpinning. An understanding of the mixed and varied approaches to learning can help you see why students react in different ways to different situations and stimuli.

Chapter 7 Caring For The Campus

We touched on just one aspect of campus provision in Chapter 3, that of the learning environment and its effects on the quality of student learning. In this final chapter, we extend that discussion to outside of classrooms and lecture theatres, looking at various aspects of the overall management and feel of the campus. Though many of the suggestions we make in this chapter will be outside the direct control of many readers of this book, we hope nonetheless that the issues we raise can be brought to the attention of those who can address them, and that everyone can play a significant part in ensuring that the issues are addressed.

We should also add that several of our suggestions in this chapter address matters that are more readily noticed by people who do not work on the campus regularly, or by people who come to the campus at off-peak times of the day, week or year. Not least among the visitors to our campuses are people serving as teaching quality assessors/reviewers, and agents of funding bodies, and the link to the importance of first impressions being good ones is obvious.

University and college campuses vary enormously. We have worked in some which seem close to learning paradises, as well as many more which are closer to the opposite! While it is often a matter of making the best of what is available, significant improvements in the quality of a campus can be made in relatively inexpensive and straightforward ways.

We begin with some practical suggestions about the often overlooked matter of helping people find their way about campuses! Perhaps indeed we should have started with an even more extensive list of suggestions about how to help strangers to find their way *to* the campus in the first instance, but some would argue that this is beyond the direct scope of this book, and in any case is a matter that can be addressed or rectified by a tiny proportion of staff in our institutions if they would only get down to it!

Our next three sets of suggestions relate to campus provision at off-peak times of the day, at weekends and during vacations. With a tendency to make more use of campus facilities during such times, it is to be expected that the concerns and solutions we raise in our exploration of these issues will gradually be addressed.

We continue with some suggestions about car parking! We feel that car parking is one rather visible barometer of the way that institutions value (and fail to value) staff, students, and visitors.

We end the book with some suggestions about another public indicator of the quality of institutions: home pages on the Internet. This is not exactly caring for the campus in the same way as other components of this chapter, but is connected with the matter of first impressions included already in this chapter. Here, our suggestions are just meant as a starting point, as the sophistication and scope of electronic publicity is changing day by day.

We are aware that this final chapter has only skimmed the surface of a wide range of issues about the quality of the working environment for staff in colleges, and the overall quality of the learning environment for students. We urge readers to look for aspects of their own campus which could be useful to place on quality enhancement agendas, when there is sufficient time and energy left over from addressing the quality of teaching, learning and assessment.

46

Helping people find their way about the campus

First impressions of a university are important, so help visitors and regular users to believe they are in a top quality environment by getting maps, signs and room numbering absolutely spot-on. People hate getting lost, and time and energy are wasted when directions are absent, opaque or confusing. These tips are designed to help universities and colleges become welcoming environments.

1 **Map the territory.** Produce maps that make it easy for people to work out where they are and where they should be. Mark easily recognisable landmarks on the maps even if they are not part of the campus, so that people can orientate themselves.

2 **Consider your campuses.** If there are several, make it very clear to everyone which campus is which. Confusion can be avoided if documentation clearly indicates this. It can be useful to have room numbers coded by campus. This can avoid someone turning up for a meeting in the right room but on the wrong campus!

3 **Indicate scale on maps, particularly if distances are great**. Where buildings are spread out over a large campus, it often surprises people how long it takes to get from one place to another – an indication that a half-mile walk is involved would be regarded as helpful!

4 **Use three-dimensional images.** It is easier to recognise buildings if you provide some approximations of what they look like, without going for total verisimilitude. Showing the highest buildings clearly on a 3-D map can be helpful for those navigating the campus. It is also useful to show the sizes and shapes of neighbouring buildings outside the campus where appropriate.

5   **Think about using technology.** Many institutions nowadays have online or CD-ROM guides to the campus, which enable visitors to walk round the campus virtually before arrival or to refer to IT guides at intervals around the buildings.

6   **Have plenty of maps of the campus**. Send them out to prospective visitors, give staff copies to send out to anyone who is arriving. Keep stocks in every building, for example in porters' lodges, so that stray visitors for other buildings can be sent confidently on their way. Consider having large-scale maps on walls and boards too, with clear indications of where the visitor is standing when reading it.

7   **Brief all your staff to welcome visitors**. Help porters, cleaners, professors and others understand that although guiding lost visitors can be tedious, especially if staff work in offices near the entrances and get lots of queries, the impression given of the institution depends on them.

8   **Sign it right.** Exterior signposts pointing to buildings are very useful for people who don't yet know which building is which, and for important visitors. The danger is that there is a feeling that 'everyone knows where the main refectory is' and so on.

9   **Sign each building carefully.** Often people spend ages looking for a building when they are right beside it, simply because it isn't clearly indicated as such. If a building changes its name, it is often a good idea to mention this somewhere, since some people still use the former name for years afterwards.

10   **Don't forget your portacabins.** These are often situated in out-of-the-way places and can be impossible to find, for example, if invisibly placed in the middle of a quadrangle. And if you move them somewhere else, make sure this is mapped and marked too.

11   **Update maps and signs regularly.** When departments move, and new buildings appear, both maps and signs can quickly become out of date. It is important that someone has the overall responsibility for monitoring this, and that new signs (even temporary ones) are installed quickly in appropriate places.

12   **Get the numbers right.** With alterations in the internal structure of buildings happening all the time, the room numbers on doors can become very confusing. Even worse, there may be no clear indications to visitors looking for a particular room about where it actually is – it has been known for Room G418 to be right at the end of a corridor, and to get to G419 from there requires a walk down two flights of stairs, across a bridge linking two parts of the building, and back up two flights!

13   **Allocate the budget**. Maps and signing are not cheap, especially if you go online. However, the price of getting it wrong or not doing it at all may be even higher in terms of lost student numbers, disgruntled users of your consultancy services and perplexed quality assessors.

14   **Walk the talk.** Use student and staff inductions as an opportunity to show people around as much as possible. Some institutions take people on a bus tour of the different campuses, while others have staff who shamelessly ham up the occasion by adopting the role of a holiday tour guide, complete with over-sized umbrella and humorous patter.

15   **Use students as guides.** Several universities use students as paid or unpaid guides to show round prospective students and to help to orientate freshers. If you decide to use students, brief them carefully and give them guidance about how to answer the ancillary questions they are likely to encounter. They usually make excellent ambassadors for your university or college.

16   **Get out and show people.** You may frequently find yourself telling someone how to proceed from one part of the campus to another, forgetting new fences have been put up recently, making your usual route impassable. Don't rely on your memory! It is useful to *take* the person at least once in a while, to check whether you may have forgotten a vital turning in the route you would have suggested.

17   **Save newcomers blushes.** It is useful to visitors and new personnel or students if signs to the nearest toilets are clearly displayed, without the route petering out. Help students who have personal or religious needs find their way to washing facilities, places to take medicine and places where they can pray.

18   **Remember the needs of people with disabilities.** It can be useful to have maps indicating routes for wheelchair users. Show clearly on maps buildings where lifts are located. Investigate the use of Braille markings or other means of helping those with visual impairments.

19 **Consider colour-coding routes**. People often find it helpful to be told to 'follow the blue line to the learning resource centre', for example, particularly where this is both indicated on the map and painted on the ground. Colour can also be used to indicate which building is which, or indeed which level one is on within a building.

20 **Think safety.** For example, in any corridor there should always be signs to a route leading to an exit which is not just an alarmed, emergency one. On badly lit or leafy campuses, don't direct people along a route that is likely to lead to them into danger.

47

Early mornings and late evenings

With greater proportions of students studying part-time, and with full-time classes increasingly timetabled over a greater part of the day than used to be the case, the population of a campus or a building is greater during early mornings and late evenings than used to be the case. Caring appropriately for this population is a significant part of the quality enhancement agenda of any institution. Some matters to address are suggested below.

1   **Make safety a priority.** There are several aspects to ensuring safety, and many of these become even more important when the buildings are only partially occupied rather than busy. For a start, it is important that however many or few staff and students are in a building, the emergency evacuation procedures must always be possible to implement effectively.

2   **Make sure people don't get locked in!** While it may be appropriate to lock people *out* of buildings or sections of a building during late evenings, it is important that any people still inside can get out without impediment. Locking doors which remain openable from the inside, but which lock after people make their exit, help to minimise such problems. However, there remains the risk that unwanted intruders enter as someone leaves.

3   **Respect people's need for personal security.** This could include ensuring that frequent (but irregular in pattern) patrols of security personnel take place, checking which rooms are still occupied during evenings, and locking or securing empty rooms to prevent undesirable intruders lurking there.

4   **Consider a personal alarm system.** There are many possibilities, including electronic devices to draw attention to (and frighten assailants away from) people walking through deserted parts of a building or campus. Wired-in alarm systems may be appropriate for parts of the campus which remain open late at night, including learning resources or computing centres.

5   **Consider the needs of people who arrive early in the morning.** It is increasingly common for staff (and students) to arrive early, sometimes to maximise their chances regarding car parking. It helps a lot if there is somewhere comfortable for them to wait until all buildings are open. A long-hours cafeteria or lounge area can help with this, and is best situated near a point of the campus that remains staffed (for example the main security office).

6   **The telephone switchboard is *always* important!** This is often the location from which emergency services would be summoned if necessary. However, it is desirable to have the switchboard staffed for as long as possible by personnel who can deal with routine enquiries, and take messages to be passed on next day when necessary. Out-of-hours enquirers are often potential students.

7   **Consider the merits of a 24-hour area.** Some institutions already have parts of libraries or computer centres open to staff and students on a continuous basis. It is important that such areas have good security arrangements, preferably live supervision or good video links to the main security base. Students tend to use such facilities at the most unexpected times of the night, especially when assignment or dissertation submission deadlines approach, and word-processing facilities are in high demand.

8   **Publicise transport arrangements.** Notices about the times of out-of-hours public transport services can minimise the time (and danger) of people waiting around for buses or trains.

9   **Throw light on any problems!** High-intensity halogen lighting is relatively inexpensive to maintain and run, and can ensure that people don't feel intimidated by shadowy paths between buildings at night. Infrared detectors can minimise the cost of running such lighting, ensuring it is only used when needed, with the additional advantage that who is moving around where can be monitored by security personnel.

10   **People can be hungry and thirsty.** When staffed catering facilities are closed, it can make a big difference if somewhere on the campus there are some vending machines that serve hot and cold drinks, and preferably something somewhat healthier than chocolate bars and crisps. It is obviously best if such machines can give change, or if a separate machine is adjacent which supplies change.

11   **People may still need to make photocopies.** Access to photocopiers which are still loaded with paper after the end of the working day can be much appreciated by staff and students alike.

12   **People still need toilet facilities.** Make sure that out-of-hours facilities are clearly signposted, and are in positions where security can be safeguarded.

48

Weekends

An aspect of quality enhancement that is too easily disregarded is that relating to the experience of students (and staff) who may be present on campus at weekends. In many colleges, a significant number of students actually live on campus. Staff increasingly call in at weekends to finish work they could not do during normal working weeks. The following suggestions may help make college premises better places to be at weekends.

1   **Continue to bear in mind all the points suggested in the previous section on 'Early mornings and late evenings'.** Many of the conditions and circumstances also apply at weekends, particularly the safety and security implications.

2   **Review the operation of those facilities which are most needed during weekends.** These normally include libraries, learning resources centres, computing facilities, and so on. Even if only selected parts or services are made available during weekends, they can make a big difference to residential students, and indeed full-time or part-time students who may wish to return to the campus at weekends.

3   **Maintain a general purpose enquiry point.** Even at weekends, it is useful if someone is available who can be a one-stop point for most enquiries. This can usefully include a dropping off point for letters and packages to be forwarded next week in the internal mail, and even for returned books after the library has closed. (It is better to get the books back even when missing the chance to collect fines for overdue loans than not to get them back at all!)

4   **Make it possible for staff to get into buildings at weekends.** Procedures vary. Some institutions open most buildings for a limited time on weekend days. Others have arrangements where access can be pre-booked and duly authorised, and staff can be signed in and signed out of buildings. Staff wanting to work at weekends should not be discouraged by procedural obstacles.

5   **Have some kind of catering provision at weekends.** Even a bank of vending machines is better than nothing. Staff (or students) who need to put in a weekend's work don't wish to have to travel miles for a bit of lunch!

6   **Put the campus to good uses at weekends.** For example, public lectures, exhibitions, conferences, demonstrations and so on; all of these can promote the image of an institution, and are often best timed to happen at weekends when car parking may be easier, and rooms and space more freely available.

7   **Have someone in charge of weekends!** Rather than just relying on those staff who work at weekends sharing out weekend work alongside weekday work, it is useful if someone has special responsibility for the overall shape of provision and arrangements at weekends, and knows the whole picture of what may be happening at any given time.

8   **Give someone the responsibility for surveying the quality of weekend provision.** Get them to draw up a checklist of the things that should be monitored, and to make a list of recommendations. Do such checks periodically and irregularly, to catch the flavour of different weekend scenarios.

9   **Work out clear directions about what to do in an emergency.** Such procedures need to be workable during weekends, and may be more dependent on someone reading an appropriate notice or poster than during the week when there is likely to be someone around who knows what to do. Make sure that the relevant information is displayed where it can be seen (for example, not in a locked building).

10   **Consider the implications of opening access to the general public.** If weekend events involve public access, responsibilities may arise which have not been anticipated. For example, there are special requirements regarding crowd control and safety if a weekend event is likely to be mobbed. Good liaison with the police and emergency services can help alert you to any such requirements.

49

Keeping things going during vacations

In most institutions, the term 'vacation' means much less now than it did some years ago. The principal difference tends to be that it is easier to find a car parking space! However, the quality of an institution depends as much in some ways on what happens during vacations as what happens when all the student population is present. The following suggestions may help colleges and universities make the most of vacations.

1   **Check that everything discussed previously under 'Early mornings and late nights' and 'Weekends' is still addressed.** As before, safety and security remain paramount, but it is equally important to look after the routine needs of the people who are present during vacations.

2   **Departments should be staffed appropriately.** There will always be some members of the teaching staff who wish to prepare for forthcoming teaching, or carry on with research work. It remains important that they still have support services, including technical staff, reprographics, computing, library, administrative, and so on.

3   **For some staff, crucial work needs to happen during vacations.** This includes, for example, admissions tutors, who may need to work very hard immediately after students' examination results become known. It is important that this work is seen to count appropriately, for example by enabling such staff to take time off during term time in compensation for their lost vacations.

4   **Explore ways of keeping services going.** Buildings still need to be maintained and cleaned, and vacations can provide the best time to undertake (in a well-planned way) maintenance and refurbishment. It is important, however, that such work can be planned appropriately so as not to conflict with conferences and other events which may be timetabled during vacations.

5   **Maintain at least some catering provision.** While it would be un-
     reasonable to expect full catering provision to continue all year round, it
     is useful if at least one catering point can remain in operation during
     vacations, and can provide a fairly comprehensive variety of service. This
     may be combined with rotating refurbishment of the various facilities on
     a campus.

6   **Libraries and computing services can make good use of vacation time.**
     There are many tasks that cannot be undertaken at the same time as full
     demand from students and staff, and it is important to enable support
     services to prepare systematically for the next period of busy service.

7   **Where possible, put residential accommodation to good use.** Depending
     on location and the suitability of residential accommodation, possibilities
     include residential full-cost courses, conferences, or letting the
     accommodation as holiday flats. Such usage can help to keep on domestic
     and support staffing, and the year-round employment prospects that this
     offers may attract better applicants for work in such services than short-
     term or temporary jobs will bring.

8   **Consider ways of providing a one-stop shop for casual enquiries.**
     Potential students or clients find it frustrating if they are sent on endless
     searches ending in locked doors or unstaffed offices during vacations. It
     is worth remembering that what may be considered vacation time in a
     college is perfectly normal business time in most of the rest of the world.

9   **Keep communications going.** Increasingly, staff (and often students too)
     wish to maintain links such as e-mail and computer conferencing. It is
     often possible for them to do this remotely from home, provided the central
     services continue to function! It is also worth making arrangements for
     those staff who wish for important-looking or urgent mail to be forwarded
     to them at home or at their holiday destinations (while continuing to
     respect the rights and wishes of those staff who wish to escape entirely
     for appropriate periods!)

10   **Don't take advantage of those staff who happen to live on campus.** For
     example, wardens of student accommodation may continue to be present,
     but will not enhance the image of quality of an institution if they
     continually have their doorbells ringing with enquiries that have nothing
     to do with their role.

50

Some suggestions about car parking

There is no second chance to make a good first impression, and in many institutions, first impressions are very much about car parking arrangements. This applies not just to visitors, and new staff, but also to prospective students. Some ways of making first impressions better are suggested below.

1   **Institutions need to be prepared to spend more on car parking provision.** It has as much to do with the institution's image as many other sources of expenditure including advertising, quality of buildings and promotional activity.

2   **Few things give a worse impression than a campus strewn with badly parked vehicles.** When roadways are cluttered with parked cars, pedestrian flow is impeded and made dangerous. The views from buildings are not enhanced by congested vehicles. When traffic seeking to park is slow moving, the amounts of noise and pollution added to a campus are significant.

3   **Car parks can be planned with environmental factors in mind.** Minimising the amount of traffic near buildings, and hiding car parking behind screens of shrubs or trees, can enhance the quality of the appearance and feel of an institution.

4   **Car parks should not be like derelict building sites.** It seems to happen too often that when an old building on a campus is demolished, it immediately becomes invaded with parked cars among the rubble. Car parks with properly finished roadways, and clearly marked parking bays do a lot to enhance the impression an institution gives visitors and regular users alike.

5   **Queuing outside a campus damages tempers!** When a main gate is staffed by people inspecting whether incoming vehicles are duly authorised, it is important that there are escape routes for vehicles which are not allowed to enter, rather than the system becoming blocked by them trying to turn round in confined spaces.

6   **Special permits can be posted to important visitors in advance.** Send them appropriate maps, with some way to guarantee them a space on the day concerned. Some institutions cone off reserved spaces with marker boards bearing the names of each booked visitor.

7   **Visitors' car parking is bound to need some supervision.** Otherwise, spaces intended for visitors become easy targets for unauthorised parking by staff or students. It is much more successful if the job belongs to one person rather than being something that no one has responsibility for at any given time. It does not take a very expensive appointment to make such things run smoothly.

8   **It can help if visitors are asked for their expected time of arrival.** If a visitor does not turn up within an hour of this, it would be reasonable to reallocate the space concerned to anyone with a need for it.

9   **Some visitors may need help with luggage.** External examiners arriving with bulky packages of scripts may very much appreciate someone to carry these from wherever the designated parking destination is to the building they will be working in.

10   **Look after visitors in bad weather.** When it is very wet, cold or windy, it can make a poor impression on visitors if their journey from wherever they are designated a parking place to their meeting venue is long or open to the elements. It is well worth making special arrangements when weather conditions are known to be poor.

11   **Make directions easy for important visitors to follow.** Of course, they should be easy for *anyone* to follow, but deficiencies often only seem to be brought to the surface when important visitors complain. Ensure that signs are easily read from a distance, and are accurate and up-to-date.

12   **Maintain footpaths.** Visitors probably remember more about the condition of the walkways than people who negotiate them every day and know where the potholes and loose flagstones are. When budgets are tight, it may be hard to find funds for something as basic as walkways, but spending on pedestrian transit tends to be a good long-term investment.

13   **Permit arrangements need to be made for staff and students with recognised disabilities.** For such people, assurance that they will be able to park may be crucial, and they may not be able to attend otherwise.

14   **Recognition should be made for staff whose job requires them to travel frequently from one site to another.** If such staff cannot be guaranteed a space when they return from one campus or travel to another, their movements can be made impossible, or considerable time wastage can be built into their normal work.

15   **Permit policies should reflect environmental claims often made in mission statements.** For example, where there is a good public transport system, staff and students should be encouraged to use it. Arrangements whereby buses stop regularly at key points on a campus can be made. A particularly attractive benefit for staff can be a free or subsidised season pass for buses or trains.

16   **When there is more demand than capacity, the available parking should be shared out equitably.** It is better to have two-day-a-week permits for some staff, than for them to have no share of the parking provision. Recognition should be made of the special needs of those staff who cannot arrive early because of childcare arrangements. One solution is to have a specially reserved area for designated permit holders who cannot arrive before a fixed time, with casual parking in such an area prevented.

17   **Car sharing should be encouraged.** There are various ways this can be done, such as reducing or abolishing charges for cars bringing more than one member of staff to campus regularly, or allocating places with sharing as one of the factors considered.

51

Quality on the Internet

We end this book with some suggestions which don't exactly fit into any of the chapters, since they overlap with just about all of them! They involve students, staff, processes, first impressions and external relations, all at the same time. There probably needs to be another book about using information technology and electronic communication to enhance the quality of higher education, but meanwhile here are a few suggestions for starters, particularly concerning the picture of quality that is fostered by electronic first impressions.

1   **First impressions can be electronic ones!** Many people now make their first impressions of higher education institutions through the Internet, and in particular, through logging on to home pages and then trying to find something more detailed that they may be looking for – or indeed through simply browsing through what is on offer.

2   **Make home pages easy to find.** There are various lists which are hot-linked to home pages, and it is worth checking that your home page is as easy to find from all of these lists. If making a home page for the University of Poppleton, it is worth making sure that links are just as easy from the word 'Poppleton' in any alphabetical list, and also from the cluster of entries that will be under 'University of...'

3   **Make your home pages simple to download.** Not everyone will be downloading them using high speed access to the Internet, so full-colour graphics can take some users too long to download, and they are likely to give up trying to get into your home page. You need to have pages which will give them enough to get them interested before there is anything that slows them down.

4   **People don't read pages that are too long.** It is important that your home page does not require scrolling time and time again to find things that people may want to access. Therefore, the home page should have a well thought out menu of hot-linked keywords, allowing people to focus on the school, department, member of staff or subject area as efficiently as you can arrange it.

5   **Information needs to be up to date, and there!** It is very frustrating for anyone looking for details of a particular department or course to get easily to the home page, but after a few further attempts to find specific information find that they are met by a message effectively saying that no information is available yet for the department or course that they are interested in.

6   **Information needs to be designed for the Internet, not just for the prospectus.** When people locate information that they want to follow up, they are likely to want to download it to their own computer or printer. If they end up having to print out several screens worth of information to capture the bit they really need, they become frustrated.

7   **Remember that the average time that most users look at any page on the Internet is measured in seconds, not minutes.** It is therefore important that the main points that are intended to be conveyed are done so efficiently. The editing and production skills relevant to electronic pages are quite different from those relevant to print-based publicity and information materials.

8   **Make the most of electronic communication.** People using the Internet are more likely to make use of dialogue boxes and opportunities to e-mail enquiries direct to schools, departments, individuals or service centres, than they are to take out paper, stamps and envelopes. It is important that the electronic addresses that are up on the Internet are ones that are maintained well, and not dead ends for enquirers.

9   **Show that the Internet is used effectively for teaching and learning.** It is important that, for example, staff don't just dump their course notes on the system electronically and expect them to be useful learning resources in such a medium. Learning materials need to be radically redesigned and reformatted to provide attractive and useful resources for learning.

10 **Students should be encouraged to use the Internet as a source for materials.** Many students need no prompting to do this, but sometimes they are not given sufficient credit for the information retrieval skills they display when searching for source material electronically. Electronic publishing is now an established part of the picture alongside journals, magazines and textual materials. One of the differences is in the extent of refereeing, and therefore the credibility or authenticity of the material, but a further important dimension is the speed with which new data or ideas can be put up on the Internet – far faster than can be achieved in published printed formats.

11 **Staff and students need relevant training and support so they can make the most of the Internet.** While it can be fun just to surf the net, and a useful learning experience in its own right, it is important that people are able to make structured use of the Internet to search sensibly and productively for information that is relevant to their teaching, learning and research.

12 **Ensure that there is a sufficiently wide critical mass of technophiles in the institution.** To create a good impression, it is useful if the institution is seen to be active in global, national or local discussion lists of electronic kinds. Therefore, there should be some members of each school, department and section who are ensuring that the institution takes its place among the community of electronic communication.

13 **It is useful to have an institutional policy on the Internet.** For example, it can be argued that every contributor to the Internet is in one way or another an ambassador of the institution, and there may need to be some sensible ground rules to protect against the institution being brought into disrepute by unsuitable contributions. This may mean some kind of vetting or monitoring of contributions, and some safeguards to ensure that they are appropriate. This may have an effect on the institution's own local regulations for the use of computing facilities.

14 **Sample course materials need to create a good impression.** Many institutions now offer some courses or programmes online, or put up sample course materials on the Internet to attract students to enrol on courses. Such materials set people's expectations regarding the standard of educational provision offered by the institution as a whole, and therefore such materials need to be checked carefully both for content and style.

Conclusions

Quality enhancement is a continuous process, but a book has to end somewhere. There are well over 500 tips already in this book, and readers who have got this far can probably think of at least another 500. You may well be thinking, 'But they haven't covered...' and 'There's not much about...' but we hope you will also be thinking, 'I liked the section on...', 'I wish I'd read this book before I started...', and 'I learned a lot about...'

If any of these are true for you, we'd love to hear from you since, in keeping with the theme of this book, we aim to continuously improve the relevance, usefulness and clarity of our writing. Every book we write receives lots of feedback at a pilot stage, and we try to incorporate this into the final version. In the case of this book most of the feedback we received during piloting was about things we should add, and we have done this. We also take note of all feedback we receive after publication and aim to use this advice to help us write the next edition or the next book. If you would like to join in, you can contact us via Kogan Page who will pass your comments on to us.

Further Reading And References

Brown, S and Pennington, R C (1995) *The Staff Developer and Quality Assessment,* University and Colleges Staff Development Agency/Staff and Educational Development Agency (UCoSDA/SEDA), Sheffield/Birmingham.

Brown, S, Rawnsley, S and Jones, G (1996) *Observing Teaching,* SEDA, Birmingham.

Colling, C *et al.* (1994) *Assessment of Quality: Guidance Notes,* University of Northumbria, Newcastle.

D'Andrea, V and Gibbs, G (1996) *Preparing for HEFCE Quality Assessment* OCSLD, Oxford.

Entwistle, N (1992) *The Impact of Teaching and Learning Outcomes in Higher Education: A Literature Review,* CVCP Universities' Staff Development Unit, Sheffield.

Harvey, L, Burrows, A and Green, D (1992) *Criteria of Quality,* University of Central England, Birmingham.

HEFCE (1995) *Quality Assessment Between October 1996 and September 1998,* Circular 26/95 (October) Higher Education Funding Council for England, Bristol.

HEFCE (1995) *Report on Quality Assessment 1992–1995,* Circular 18/95 (November), Higher Education Funding Council for England, Bristol.

HEFCE (1996) *Assessors' Handbook,* 2nd edn, Higher Education Funding Council for England, Bristol.

NATFHE (1992) A Question of Quality, London, NATFHE, London.

UCoSDA and Loughborough University (1996) *Making the Grade: Achieving High Quality Assessment Profiles,* UCoSDA, Sheffield.

Index